Tread Softly
For You Tread On My Life

Tread Softly
For You Tread On My Life

New & Collected Writings
MICHAEL KING

CAPE CATLEY LTD

For C.K. Stead
who, like execution,
concentrates the mind.

First published July 2001
Second printing July 2001
Cape Catley Ltd
Ngataringa Road
P O Box 32-622
Devonport, Auckland
New Zealand

Email: cape.catley@xtra.co.nz
Visit our website: www.capecatleybooks.co.nz

Copyright Michael King 2001

Typeset in Sabon
Designed and typeset by Kate Greenaway, Auckland
Cover photo by Reg Graham
Cover by Christine Cathie Design, Auckland
Printed by Publishing Press Ltd, Auckland.

ISBN: 0-908561-88-1

&

Contents

&

Introduction

$\mathcal{M}$Y FRIEND AND COLLEAGUE, novelist Maurice Shadbolt, once impressed upon me that it was the responsibility of the writer to be at all times alert with suspicion of the existing social and economic orders. In support of this, he quoted what John Steinbeck said in Stockholm in 1962 as he received his Nobel Prize for Literature. "The writer is charged with exposing our many grievous faults and failures, and with dredging up to the light our dark and dangerous dreams."

As an historian, I have to say that such an imperative does not always sit easily with the call to be fair-minded. I also recall that, less than a year after issuing this prescription to me, Shadbolt — a staunch republican — was delighted to be made a Commander of the Most Excellent Order of the British Empire. We each have our own ways of coming to terms with history.

It seems to me, though, that History with a capital H *does* have something more to offer society than simply chastisement for our inevitable failures to live up to ideals and expectations. I think of something John Dos Passos wrote in *The Ground We Stand On*. "In times of change," he said, "when there is a quicksand of fear under people's reasoning, a sense of continuity with generations gone before can stretch like a lifeline across an alarming present."

"A sense of continuity . . ." That's one stabilising and fortifying effect of *known* history, and one that is eminently usable and useful. But I would go further than this. Arthur Schlesinger Jnr asserts that a knowledge and an understanding of the past give the present a new sense of purpose, possibility and dignity. What he is saying, I think, is that the historian has at least the *potential* to absorb the past, identify in it what is of continuing importance by way of values and experience, and then to communicate these things to a contemporary audience by way of saying, "This is what we've done that we can be proud of — or *not* proud of; these are the values of our forebears that provide helpful signposts for future directions and behaviour". In this way good history absorbs the past, but at the same time creates new orientations for the present and foreshadows the future.

It is in this spirit and belief that the following pieces were written. All of them are what Richard Holmes calls "wanderings from the main path", sidetracks that arose in the course of other, larger, historical and biographical expeditions. But, as Holmes also says, quoting Shakespeare's Polonius, it is by indirections that we find out directions.

These pieces, then, are reflections that arose from the writing of history and biography; and, in particular, they represent a search for the modest signposts towards meaning and understanding — to say nothing of entertainment — with which those genres engage and reward us. And they emphasise, I hope, that there is nothing as singular in all the world and as variable and as interesting as human behaviour.

Michael King

&

Tread Softly —
Biography and Compassionate Truth

First presented at a Stout Research Centre seminar in February 1997; and published subsequently in New Zealand Studies, *Vol. 8, No. 2, September 1998.*

*B*IOGRAPHERS CAN'T HELP BUT BE AWARE that some of their potential subjects are terrified of the genre. As Sir Charles Wetherell remarked, biography adds a new zone of horror to the business of getting dead and being dead.

One only has to reflect on the delight with which biographers fall upon inappropriate, or — even worse — appropriate, last words: Florence Nightingale's, "I smell something burning," for example; or Nancy Astor's, "Am I dying or is it just my birthday?"

Consider the formerly stainless reputations of men such as Gordon of Khartoum and Lord Kitchener besmirched by writers with a fraction of their subject's talent, panache or experience; pontifications on what decisions the biographee *ought* to have made in the heat of battle, politics or relationships; disclosures of a prurient nature about unusual sexual proclivities; revelations that the Revered Public Figure, loved by all who came into contact with him professionally, was a tyrant and a bully at home. (I hasten to add that I am not being sexist in my choice of examples and pronouns. The conventions laid down by the practitioners of English Victorian biography ensure that the inflated reputations so perforated by twentieth century biographers are almost entirely those of men.)

Of this, the more tawdry aspect of modern biography, Janet Malcolm notes: "It is the medium through which the remaining secrets of the famous are taken from them and dumped in full view of the world. The biographer at work, indeed, is like the professional burglar, breaking into a house, rifling through certain drawers that he has good reason to believe contain the jewellery and money, and triumphantly bearing his loot away . . . The more the biography reflects the biographer's industry, the more the reader believes that he or she is having an elevating literary experience, rather than simply listening to backstairs gossip and reading other people's mail."

Is it any wonder that as distinguished and experienced a biographer as New Zealand's Antony Alpers — who knew the score on such matters — announced that he planned to destroy his family papers on the basis that copyright laws were insufficient to preserve reputations. "Under the present New Zealand Copyright Act, all copyright protection is withdrawn from unpublished writings only seventy-five years after the author's death," he wrote in *Confident Tomorrows*, an anthology of his father's writings. 'Unauthorised copies can then be exploited by anyone for any purpose. Against that odious possibility the destruction of private papers alone can give full protection.'

What provoked this threat to destroy biographical evidence — and this from a man whom some would identify as New Zealand's most distinguished biographer? His letters to me suggest that he was affronted by the spectacle of no-holds-barred biographies, possibly including his own latter one on Katherine Mansfield, in which it is assumed that there is no longer any meaningful distinction to be drawn between public and private lives; and in which it is further assumed that anything a subject has left evidence of doing is a legitimate object for the voyeurism of biographers and readers.

One supposes that Alpers was mindful of the group of so-called Bloomsbury biographies, which more than any others challenged what had previously been the boundaries of acceptability and good taste: those on Lytton Strachey, Virginia Woolf, Vanessa Bell, John Maynard Keynes, Bertrand Russell, Ottoline Morrell, and others. He may also have been thinking of what is in the process of becoming a tradition of current American biography: not simply a frankness about subjects' private lives but a considerable degree of coarseness as well (and who, having read it, can forget Robert Caro's description of Lyndon Baines Johnson forcing his staff to talk with him while he was defecating and inspecting his own ordure?)

Eighty years have elapsed since Lytton Strachey remarked that discretion was *not* the better part of biography. But what Strachey regarded as publishable indiscretion wilts like candy-floss before a bonfire in comparison with biographical texts of the late twentieth century. And so it is worth asking: are there or should there be ground rules for biographers in this area? Should any facts about a subject's life be regarded by the biographer as being beyond justifiable scrutiny? And, if so, should this be out of consideration for the biographee, the biographee's family and associates, or readers?

In relation to readers, one is inescapably reminded of those warnings on television in which 'viewer discretion' — whatever that may be — 'is advised.' Should biographies carry similar warnings? I think not. In the relatively open societies that make up Western countries and their cultures we can — in this context at least — disregard the welfare of readers. They must be subject to the *caveat emptor* proviso that applies to all purchasable commodities. And if they expect to be damaged or unduly shocked by a biography they can snap it shut or choose not to open it.

Let me refer to the other parties in the equation, however — the biographee, and the biographee's family and friends — because they do, I believe, have rights which the ethical biographer ought to take into consideration.

Given that one of the major and wholly legitimate aims of biography is to re-create the life of the subject, to assess such things as character, motivation and mannerism, and to set the subject in the context of his or her times, then almost everything known about a biographee's life that furthers these aims is justifiable grist to the biographer's mill — provided the subject is dead. Live subjects are in a different category and I shall refer to them separately.

A biographer writing about dead subjects decides to withhold or overlook evidence on two grounds.

One is where that evidence suggests behaviour so far out of character with other evidence that it is highly suspect. One informant insisted to me that Frank Sargeson had stolen jewellery from him. This was wholly at odds with other evidence, which showed consistently Sargeson's lack of interest in material possessions and his inclination to give away money or luxury items on the rare occasions he had them. Any doubts I may have had on the matter were dissolved when a member of the informant's family warned me that he was a liar, and cited other instances when that same person had invented anecdotes about other events which had never occurred.

All biographers encounter such stories. They are not rejected on grounds of prejudice or taste, but as part of an informed evaluation made in the context of other evidence; as part of the biographer's conscientious pursuit of what actually occurred.

The other category of evidence that may be withheld is that relating to sexual behaviour. Sex has the potential to pose problems for biographers when they ask of evidence: is this relevant? It is a problem because almost everybody is interested in sex and there is consequently a temptation to use all such material in the legitimate pursuit of an engaging narrative. It is also a problem because the relationship of sexuality to the rest of life is profound; but the process of measuring that relationship in individual lives, and ascribing cause and effect, is an exceedingly inexact science.

In the case of Sargeson, I made an early decision simply to treat his homosexuality the way I would have dealt with heterosexuality. And that judgment alone solved some potential problems of selectivity. I also adopted a useful maxim of David Marr, Patrick White's biographer, that the biographer has the right to go as far as the bedroom but not as far as the bed — in other words, to convey the nature of the biographee's sexuality and indicate who sexual partners were; but not to describe the mechanics of sexual acts. By chance, I *did* know what kind of sexual acts Sargeson liked and disliked. But I believed that this category of information was the business of Sargeson and his sexual partners, not that of the biographer or readers.

The analogy with heterosexuality is not *quite* the whole story, however. Clearly, being homosexual at a time when the society in which you live generally abhors homosexual acts, and despatches the guardians of the law to snoop and pry in search of evidence of such acts, and sends you to prison if you are caught committing them — all this made life perilous for active homosexuals and imposed stresses to which heterosexual people were not subject. It led Sargeson to refer to homosexuality, in conversation and in writing, in an oblique and allusive way; and that habit of obliqueness infiltrated other areas of his life.

I had also to deal with the enduring and pervasive effects of his conviction in 1929 for indecent assault on a male — an episode which turned out to be crucial to an understanding of his decision to stay with his uncle on a King Country farm for eighteen months, and to change his name. In other words, sexuality affects far wider areas of life than the simple committing or the nature of sexual acts.

Next I come to the question of the biographee's surviving relatives and friends. In the past I have quoted with approval a maxim of Voltaire's: "To the living one owes respect; to the dead one owes the truth." It is true that nothing one says about the dead, true or false, positive or negative, can affect them; it is also true that the dead cannot take action for libel or defamation — and some less than scrupulous biographers have capitalised on this to invent allegations about their subject or to purvey rumours and half-truths as if they were verified or verifiable information. These are frequently the characteristics of unauthorised celebrity biographies.

I should stress here, perhaps, that I take it as axiomatic that any biographer with aspirations towards professionalism is in the business of seeking truth as it emerges from verifiable evidence and not that of inventing facts. I also take it as axiomatic that the scholar has a duty — as far as possible — to tell the truth about the dead subject's character and motivations. Should that duty be in any way limited or constrained by the first part of Voltaire's maxim, "to the living one owes respect . . ."? Are there facts about a biographee's life that might unjustifiably hurt or offend relatives or associates? And should information about such matters be withheld? My answer to both questions would have to be a qualified Yes, there might be . . .

Frank Sargeson had no spouse or offspring, and that to some extent made discussion of his sexual life a more straightforward task than it might have been. Further, homosexuality had been decriminalised for a decade in New Zealand by the time I came to publish the biography. He did have two surviving siblings, sisters; but they had long since come to terms with the nature of their brother's love life.

Sargeson's partner Harry Doyle, on the other hand, had relatives who were anything but relaxed about the relationship between the two men. I made strenuous efforts to contact them prior to publication of the book. Since they were almost all, by this time, female, and their surnames were no longer Doyle, it was a difficult task and one that I eventually abandoned. Soon after the biography appeared, however, I received a letter from a niece of Doyle. It was addressed to me and asked me to tell the Sargeson Trust that if Harry Doyle's name was ever again mentioned publicly in connection with that of Frank Sargeson, "there would be consequences". The warning was underlined.

Their objection was that Doyle was revealed publicly as homosexual. Had I known of this feeling before publication, I would probably not have changed anything I said in the book. I had written about the Sargeson-Doyle relationship with care and, I hoped, sensitivity. But I felt I owed it to the Doyle family to do what I had done in the case of the Sargeson family: to prepare them for what was to appear in print; and to show them what I proposed to say so that I could give due consideration to any reservations or suggestions they had prior to publication. That would have been how I exercised "respect for the living" in this instance.

In a climate in which homosexual acts were now decriminalised, however, and in which public attitudes towards them had changed considerably since the time of Doyle's death in 1971, I would not have been prepared to exclude discussion of the fact that the Sargeson-Doyle relationship had been, among other things, homosexual. Besides, Sargeson himself had already made reference to the fact in print, albeit in oblique terms, in his autobiography; anybody with a degree of nous would have understood from that text that he was connected to Doyle sexually.

When I published a biography of the late Dame — indeed, the Great Dame — Whina Cooper in 1983, I withheld information that would have been a source of embarrassment and distress to her had it been published in her lifetime. The higher you rise in public esteem, the further you have to fall if your *curriculum vitae* is found to contain evidence of less than creditable behaviour. And the Mother of the Nation did some highly questionable things long before she knew that she would come to be regarded as worthy of this title.

Three years after her death I would still withhold this information. Not out of concern for Whina, who is now subject to the judgment of a higher court, but out of continuing consideration for her family. The knowledge that the canvassing of certain episodes would cause *them* embarrassment and distress is sufficient to constrain me, because that constraint is how in this instance I exercise respect for the living.

There is more to the equation than this consideration alone, however.

These same family members have assisted me, ransacked their recollections and their attics for information and documents, persuaded otherwise reluctant witnesses to talk to me, and offered me frequent and warm hospitality — which I have accepted. Some might say — indeed, *have* said in the case of Michael Bassett's biography of Gordon Coates — that acceptance of co-operation and hospitality of this kind compromises biographers, because their primary focus then moves from the pursuit of truth to the maintenance of good relations with informants. There is some truth to this allegation. Acceptance of such assistance implies a trade-off: an assumption that biographers are unlikely to bite the hands that feed them by publishing information of a damaging character.

Alongside that factor, however, one should place two others. The first is that the biographer may have decided to withhold such information, anyway, as part of the "respect for the living" consideration. And the second is that the co-operation of family and associates enables biographers to locate and make use of a range of evidence that might not otherwise have been available to them, to speak with people who might have held their peace, and to have copyright clearance to quote extensively from the biographee's writings and make use of his or her photographs. A denial of these opportunities, particularly in a country the size of New Zealand, could mean that the range of material available to the biographer would be too thin to justify the writing of a book-length study.

Clearly, I am identifying and commending a trade-off in which the biographer gives away some rights; but in doing so gains access to materials and opportunities that enrich and enhance the resulting text.

Circumstances which may cause a writer to hesitate to publish evidence, at least in a primary biography written within decades of the subject's life, include instances (or the effects) of alcohol abuse, incest, illegitimacy, insanity and suicide. Anne Stevenson, one of several biographers of Sylvia Plath, wrote: 'Any biography of Sylvia written during the lifetimes of her family and friends must take their vulnerability into consideration, even if completeness suffers as a result.' I agree. But I note also with concern that Stevenson was pilloried as a consequence of this scrupulousness and accused of having sold her integrity as a scholar in exchange for the regard of Ted Hughes, his sister and his children.

Almost every biographer at some time encounters instances that create dilemmas of this kind. Even to discuss them in anything like specific terms is to draw attention to the very factors one has agreed not to make public, out of consideration for the feelings, and possibly even the physical or mental health, of those affected. One can say no more — except to affirm that there are times when revelation of previously unknown circumstances can precipitate problems of a far more serious nature than a temporary gap in the historical record.

In the case of a biography of a living person the equation changes from that which applies to dead subjects: because the laws of defamation do apply, and because the biographee becomes one of those to whom the biographer owes respect in addition to truth (unless one is setting out to write a wholly debunking book).

The objects of biography in this instance do not change.

With living subjects the biographer is still trying to locate them in their social, cultural and historical contexts; one is still trying to indicate to readers what makes the biographee 'tick'; one is still trying to shed light on motivation and character, and to identify and evaluate achievement.

But one is trying to accomplish these objectives within certain constraints. One aims at what writer and publisher Christine Cole Catley has called "compassionate truth": a presentation of evidence and conclusions that fulfil the major objectives of biography, but without the revelation of information that would involve the living subject in unwarranted embarrassment, loss of face, emotional or physical pain, or a nervous or psychiatric collapse.

Here too the biographer may enter into an implied or explicit contract of the kind I mentioned before. In return for not revealing the sorts of things living subjects might regard as inappropriate in their lifetime — and the nature of these circumstances might well vary from subject to subject — the biographer may be given access to a wide body of evidence that only the biographee can release; and, in most instances, permission to quote from the published or unpublished writings of the biographee, a huge advantage in the case of literary biography.

Although the biographer may feel at times restrained and restricted by such an arrangement, the compensations from a literary and scholarly viewpoint almost always outweigh the disadvantages. 'Compassionate truth' implies working from the record and following evidence to whatever conclusions it indicates; but having at the same time regard for the sensibilities of living people, including the biographee, who may be characters in this narrative. And that consideration conditions *what* evidence is cited and *how* it is cited, and what conclusions are reached and how they are expressed.

The whole process is analogous to tightrope walking. But the resulting tension frequently tightens one's narrative and increases its vibrancy. And the additional balance that can result from communication and trust between biographer and biographee can achieve worthwhile professional objectives.

Which is not to suggest that a biography of — say — Janet Frame published in the year 2000 would be the same as one published in 2050. It could not be. Even apart from the greater freedom to publish which inevitably follows the deaths of all protagonists, the questions asked and the themes selected by another biographer in another era would be different. In this sense, subjects deserving of biography never die: they go on growing and changing with the interests and perceptions of successive generations of readers. Hence, as Virginia Woolf said, biographies of major figures need to be rewritten for each generation.

There is nevertheless much of value that *can* and *should* be said in the writing and publication of that initial 'primary' biography. Antony Alpers, speaking in a very different context from the one I quoted previously, and mindful of his *two* biographies of Katherine Mansfield, saw the business of biography as a continuous process rather than the sporadic publication of individual books:

"That process may be spread over decades . . . [and] leads to the emergence of an historical view of rather more than the subject alone; and this is merely set in motion by the book that I have called the primary biography. That book has to be followed by books from later writers . . ."

Indeed. And it may also be the task of later writers to colonise the narrative and analytical spaces left vacant by the primary biographer. And in this manner compassionate truth is, eventually, compatible with and complemented by the dispassionate and disinterested variety.

&

The Road to Oamaru

A talk given at the International Festival of the Arts, Wellington, in March 2000, where the author was enjoined to speak about writing the biography of Janet Frame, but not about the book itself, which was still five months away from publication.

*J*ANET FRAME IS NEW ZEALAND'S most celebrated and least public author. In a writing career that spans more than fifty years she has had published twelve novels, four story collections, one collection of poetry and three volumes of autobiography. Her work is in print in English in New Zealand, Australia, the United Kingdom and the United States; and in foreign language editions in France, Germany, Italy, Spain, Holland, Hungary, Poland, Norway, Sweden, Denmark, China and Japan.

The quality of that work, as Elizabeth Alley has noted, has moved from simple excellence to what is now recognised as something even greater. Harvard librarian and critic John Beston has called her "the most distinguished woman writer in English"; Michael Holroyd described her three volumes of memoirs as "one of the great autobiographies written this century"; Nobel Laureate Patrick White said that Frame's fiction made him feel "that I have always been a couple of steps from where I wanted to get in my own writing." Frame herself is frequently spoken of as a potential Nobel recipient and was one of six writers shortlisted for the Literature prize in 1998.

And yet despite — or because of — this reputation, Frame's reluctance to be seen or heard is legendary, comparable with that associated with J D Salinger and Thomas Pynchon. Frame declines interviews and public appearances as a matter of course. According to one journalist, on one of the rare occasions a publisher persuaded her to submit to a newspaper interview, Frame insisted that she sit in a sealed room and that questions be slid under the door to her; she then returned written answers in the same manner. That story, on investigation, turns out to be wildly exaggerated. But it is characteristic of what is said, written and believed about Frame.

Patrick Evans, one of several critics who have tried previously to write a Frame biography, noted:

"[Most] writers would do anything to be embalmed in a literary critical work that is part of a worldwide series. Frame, it seems, would do anything to avoid it. . . . By helping myself to her life I had . . . seemed [to her] like a cheerfully insensitive do-gooder barging into the house of her fiction and throwing windows open, hurling sheets into the washing machine, plumping up cushions and vacuuming the stairs whilst singing songs from the shows. . . .

"Writers who hide away probably do so principally because they want to avoid meeting people like me; and this is something Janet Frame has done with great skill and cunning. Over the years she has turned me into a sort of critical *paparazzo* . . . always trying for that special, authentic shot as I stumble through the shrubbery of her life. . . . My attempts to find first-hand information, most recently last year, have been vigorously and efficiently rebuffed, and as I have moved closer and closer to people who knew her, the less and less is said. There is a remarkable taboo around Janet Frame, a remarkable desire to protect her from enquiry."

How, then, against this background of reticence, did I come to write a Frame biography? Begin at the beginning, the old adage tells us; but of course has nothing to say about *which* beginning. The one I shall choose, on *this* occasion, is Petone, 1975. I was living with my friend Ruth Brassington in a Victorian house high on the Korokoro hill, surrounded by mature pines and macrocarpas and a great deal of wuthering. I was writing my first commissioned book, the biography of Te Puea Herangi. Ruth was working in the Cuba Mall branch of London Books, under the benign eyes of, in those days, three Mr Emmanuels.

In those (for me) relatively impoverished times, it seemed that the advantages of having friends in bookshops outweighed those of friends in high places: they were involved in the ordering of books, they were the first to see those that came in from the United Kingdom, and they were able to buy at staff discount. The consequence for us at that time was that we got to see and to read and to own exactly the kinds of books that we wanted, and to do so ahead of most of our friends and contemporaries.

It was in this congenial climate that Ruth bought me two books as presents that year: the biography of Virginia Woolf by Woolf's nephew, Quentin Bell; and that of Lytton Strachey by Michael Holroyd. To say that these books opened my eyes would be an understatement. I was already, as a reader, hooked on the genre of biography. Biographies were about people, real people; and they used human lives to open windows on subjects, countries and cultures that, through other genre, were far more difficult to enter and to comprehend.

But there was more. As a would-be writer I was already discovering the advantages of biography's in-built narrative structure: beginning, middle and end. And now, as a result of Ruth's gifts of the early Bloomsbury biographies, I could see plainly the peculiar advantages, for the biographer, of literary biography.

Writers, or at least writers of that time and place, wrote more about their own lives than non-writers. In letters and journals, but especially letters, they generated tsunamis of words about what they were thinking and feeling and doing at precisely dated times. And, because they were often morally and ethically and intellectually more adventurous than most of their contemporaries, *what* they were thinking and feeling and doing was of considerable narrative interest to other writers and to readers.

The Strachey biography was also especially important for shifting the frontiers of what was acceptable and unacceptable in biography. In this book Michael Holroyd made an incontrovertible case for the notion that private lives have a bearing on public lives; and, in the particular case of Lytton Strachey, that being homosexual at a time when homosexual acts were outlawed was about far more than simply what one did in bed with partners of one's choice.

For me at that time, however, the overwhelming advantage apparent from those two books, and the ones that followed about other members of the Bloomsbury set, was the wide range of evidence that such characters left of their intellectual lives, in addition to their more quotidian activities. The life I was researching and writing about at that time, Te Puea's, bore a close resemblance to that of a whale observed from a whaling ship: every now and then the object of the chase surfaced and blew, often in unexpected places; but then it sounded and disappeared again. What was going on in the vasty depths, where all the behavioural and motivational decisions were being made?

Literary biography, it seemed to me, offered more real and more substantial possibilities for investigating the vasty depths of the human psyche than the lives of non-literary subjects. I noted the fact, determined to write a literary biography for my next book, then got on with the job at hand.

In December 1976, I had completed the Te Puea biography in Menton, on the Katherine Mansfield Fellowship. My host and patron in that congenial Cote d'Azur town, Anton Vogt, asked me what was next. I said that I wanted to write a biography of James K. Baxter. Why? I rattled off what I had come to see as the advantages of literary biography, at least for the biographer; and I added that Baxter was probably the most interesting person I had met up to that time.

Tony Vogt, who — it occurred to me later — was almost certainly of the opinion that *he* was the most interesting person I had met up to that time, was not enthusiastic. "I don't think you should do Baxter," he said. "I think Vincent O'Sullivan should do Baxter." (I had just given him O'Sullivan's book on Baxter in the Oxford University Press New Zealand writers and their work series.) "O'Sullivan understands Baxter better than you ever will. I think you should write about Janet Frame."

"Why?" I asked in turn.

"Because she's a genius," Vogt said. "And she's the most important writer New Zealand has ever produced and possibly *will* ever produce. And besides," he went on, "I know a few things about Janet."

And then he told me some stories that were, at that time, "inside" knowledge: how John Money had brought Janet's *Lagoon* stories to him in 1947, and he, Vogt, had recommended that they go to Caxton Press for publication; how he had been one of the judges of the Hubert Church Award in 1952, which had given the prize to Frame for those same stories, now published, and thus saved her from a leucotomy at Seacliff Hospital; how he had defended *Owls Do Cry* against an unfavourable review in the *Listener*, and been ridiculed by Bill Oliver when he called it "one of the great novels of the century" (Bill Oliver had referred to this judgment as "another one of Mr Vogt's disastrous enthusiasms"); and, finally, how he and his wife Birgitte had rescued Janet from a cupboard-sized apartment in Menton in 1974 and put her in their own rental accommodation.

I listened to all this attentively. I knew who Janet Frame was. I had a copy of *The Lagoon and other Stories* in the beautifully produced 1961 edition; and I had read *Owls Do Cry, Faces in the Water* and *The Edge of the Alphabet*; and then I had sworn off Frame, because I had found the novels dark and troubling. I could see the merit in what Tony Vogt was saying, but I was not interested in Janet Frame as a subject for biography, because I was not *engaged* by her life or her work. I was, however, engaged by everything I knew about Jim Baxter.

Consequently, when I returned to Wellington I wrote to Jacquie Baxter, the poet's widow, and asked if I could be, and could be *designated*, Jim's biographer. Her letter in reply was prompt, polite and short. She thanked me for my interest; and informed me that Father Frank McKay was already at work on a James K Baxter biography, with her blessing.

I was enormously disappointed. But the same week I received that letter, Christine Cole Catley introduced me to Alister McIntosh, who thought that he might want help writing a book of memoirs. That meeting led to my beginning, and then not finishing, a life of Peter Fraser (it has since been completed by Michael Bassett, and published as a jointly authored book in March 2001). Fraser, like Te Puea, had turned out to be another whale: throughout his entire life cycle, he was visible, and traceable, only at widely spaced intervals.

Then followed some more Maori books, some non-Maori ones, and biographies of Whina Cooper and Andreas Reischek. As a writer, I was unable to activate my interest in literary biography until the Sargeson Trust agreed in 1990 to let me write the life of Frank Sargeson. And I might say, at this point, that they did not "commission" me to write it, because one member of the trust was a self-described "intellectual free marketeer". There must be no suggestion that I had "exclusive" rights to Sargeson's story, he said; and if somebody else popped up and proposed to do another biography of Sargeson at the same time, then the vigour and the rigour of the competition would be good for both writers and for the end products. I was not in accord with this view. But in the end there was no competitor, largely because one potential biographer had the grace to withdraw.

Meantime, in the wake of the Menton fellowship, I had met Frank Sargeson, interviewed him, and heard some of *his* stories about Janet Frame. And, in 1978, I had met Janet herself, as a consequence of PEN offering her some assistance. That was at her home in Gonville, Wanganui, where she was already under siege from the kind of neighbourhood noise that drove her from house to house, and town to town, over a period of nearly thirty years.

The following year, I was instrumental in persuading her to attend the 1979 writers' conference organised by PEN and the English Department of Victoria University. Any sense of triumph we might have felt at this coup was dashed the moment she walked into her first conference session. It was on Maori and Polynesian writing, chaired by Bill Parker. As Janet came in late, with Jacquie Baxter, and took a seat at the back of the lecture theatre, the chairman rose to his feet and said to the audience, "Ladies and gentlemen, I would ask you all to put your hands together and welcome our guest of honour, Janet Frame." The audience did as requested, and turned its collective head to look at the far back corner of the room. The guest of honour got to her feet and walked out, followed by a disappointed-looking Jacquie Baxter. And we never saw her again that weekend.

In the succeeding years I called in to see Janet whenever I travelled by car up or down the North Island: at Levin, and later in Palmerston North. Over this time I read the rest of her oeuvre, and found that what I had previously experienced as a veil of gloom seemed to lift in her later novels; or that, possibly, I as a reader was maturing as I worked my way through them. As I did so, other qualities I had not been aware of previously, including humour, and an apparently deliberate deflation of expectation, came closer to the forefront. Like most of the readers and admirers of her fiction, I was continually astonished by her ability to find metaphors for subtleties of human behaviour and experience that had largely eluded other writers. And I loved the way she seemed to rinse the words she used and thus made the colours of her prose and poetry new and vivid. I also thought that *Living in the Maniototo* and *The Carpathians* were among the most engrossing and interestingly complex books I had ever read.

And then, of course, there were the autobiographies: startlingly sharp evocations of her own life, which turned out to have widespread resonance for readers around the world, whose sole common denominator was their human nature. My admiration for these books was qualified only by the fact that, for the three years of their publication, they cleaned up the very same non-fiction prizes for which I, by now a professional writer of non-fiction, was competing. On two of those occasions, judges' reports informed me that I was runner-up to yet another superb volume of autobiography by our most distinguished writer. I confess to an element of relief when Frame announced, after the third volume, that the work was a trilogy and she planned to return to the writing of fiction.

As a potential Frame biographer, I also felt that Frame had by now done the job herself, and that there would be no further room for or interest in a Frame biography for a very long time. And I continued to visit her periodically — once, memorably, in Palmerston North when, according to my recollection, she asked if I would do her a favour. Of course. What was it? Her car, a Daihatsu Charade — what else for our most sly writer of fiction? — was in the driveway. She had had it serviced, and the mechanic had returned it here. Would I put it out on the street for her? Certainly, but why? "Well," said Janet, "I have my licence, of course. But I prefer to organise things so that I only have to drive forwards." Ah! I thought later, a potential biography title: *Forever Forwards* . . .

I was a member of the Sargeson Trust when Janet was appointed first resident Sargeson Fellow in 1987; and I was invited to the dinner which the British Council put on for her at Orsini's Restaurant in Wellington on the evening of the day she was invested as a member of the Order of New Zealand and handed the Commonwealth Literature Prize by the Queen — invited, that is, but unable to attend. But that same year, 1990, I began to write a biography of Frank Sargeson and Janet was a considerable help. She not only remembered, with near-total recall, events of her stay with Sargeson in 1955-56; she also remembered almost all the stories Frank had told her over this period about other episodes in his life; and, of course, she continued to see him and to correspond with him until his death in 1982. She turned out to be a major source of information for the biography, regarding her co-operation, I think, as an act of filial piety. I interviewed her, corresponded with her, and discussed with her drafts of relevant chapters.

By August 1995 I was nearing the close of the Sargeson biography and, inevitably, giving consideration to what I might do next. By this time I was further convinced of the merits of literary biography in terms of those features I had first detected in the Bloomsbury books. While it was never possible to burrow *completely* inside the human psyche of another, or to re-create how that other was seeing and feeling and thinking about the world, one came closest to an intimate kind of viewpoint in the case of people who left an ample sufficiency of *evidence* of their inner lives. Because their business was the production of words and the endless recycling of their own experience, writers came closer than other kinds of people to generating such evidence and leaving it potentially accessible to other writers.

I had now decided that, in an ideal world, I would indeed like to write a biography of Janet Frame, and for all the reasons Tony Vogt had proposed twenty years before. In particular, I too was now convinced that she was our most able writer, and the one in whom public interest would remain most enduring. I kept stumbling across quotations about other writers that seemed to have application to Janet and to keep pointing me in her direction: like Robertson Davies' comment that some writers produce work that, like wine, is so rich in fruitiness and aftertaste and hence survives them; and William Maxwell's remark about Flaubert who, he said, wrote "with infinite labour, infinite patience, and infinite thought for the technical aspects of what he was creating, none of which must show in the final draft". Such writers, he said, "go straight to heaven . . . and their books are not forgotten."

I was also aware, however, of Janet's profound distaste for public disclosure of facts about her own life, particularly disclosures made by others. She was deeply convinced that what mattered, and what people had a right to see and know, were the published writings that an author chose to release into the public domain. The rest was private, the business only of the individual, and of the individual's friends and family. And, in Janet's case, those friends and family had developed a deeply ingrained habit of *non*-disclosure of information about her.

While Janet had initially, almost reluctantly, written an autobiography that covered half her life, she had done so only to have what she referred to as "my say". And she was driven to it by what she felt were the impertinent and wildly inaccurate versions of parts of her life that others had written and published. She wanted to set the "record" straight; and in particular she wanted to dispel the notion that she was a genius whose art arose from a disordered mind. I think she also believed, erroneously, as it turned out, that, if she wrote an autobiography, it would quench what appeared to be the public's insatiable thirst for information about her life, and dry up the pool of *other* people determined to write about it.

Alas! Her three volumes of autobiography acted like petrol on the flames of curiosity and fanned an even larger bonfire of interest. Now, not only did people still want to write speculatively about her life but she also discovered she had spawned a new and largely academic industry devoted to analysis of her autobiographies, and to questions such as to what extent were they "true" or misleading; and were they written deliberately to conceal more than they reveal. One critic even went so far as to suggest that they may have been devised to cover some skeleton in the oedipal closet.

All this I more or less knew in 1995, because we had talked about the business of biography and autobiography in the context of Sargeson's life. I was not wholly hopeful, therefore, when I wrote to Frame in August of that year and asked if she would consider designating me her biographer and helping me to write such a book. I would have been even less hopeful if I had known that she had written earlier that same year to Elizabeth Alley, her executor, and said that the very thought of being "biographied" was like a beetle crawling on her skin.

As things transpired, she replied that I should come to Palmerston North to discuss the matter with her. I made that trip, imagining that I would have to marshal evidence and arguments to persuade her that what I was proposing was a good idea, for her as well as for me. And what would have made that conversation difficult was the fact that even *I* wasn't convinced that it was a good idea for *her*, other than as a means to further clear away misunderstandings and to put off other people whom I knew had been presenting themselves to her, or to her publishers and agent, as biographer-candidates.

I arrived at her house in Dahlia Street, weighed down by what I imagined would be the gravity and the difficulty of the encounter, and by no means confident of my ability to make my case in ways that would move her. Janet opened the door and, before I had even had an opportunity to greet her, said, "Yes." I said, "Yes what?" She said, "Yes, you can do the book." I said, "Then what have I come here to discuss?" And she said, "How we go about it, how exactly we do it." And that was a topic to which I had as yet scarcely turned my mind.

Unbeknown to me, various people, including Elizabeth Alley and her American publisher, George Braziller, had been urging Frame to "appoint" a biographer for the very reason that had occurred to me: so that she would have a means of putting an end to the stream of requests and inquiries on that topic. Doing so would also give her a degree of input into and control over the process, they said, which would be entirely lacking if biographies were written without her authorisation. Janet herself worried that if a non-New Zealander were to do such a book, they might not fully understand the New Zealand dimension of her life, what it meant to be the child of a railways family, for example. The result was that by the time I arrived at Dahlia Street in August 1995 she had made her decision. And one way of characterising that decision would be to call it a case of opting for professional cohabitation with a devil she knew rather than risk that with devils she knew not.

I did have a moment of doubt about the validity of her decision. That was in January 2000, when I read that Gore Vidal had authorised Fred Kaplan to write *his* biography, under the impression that he was *Justin* Kaplin, biographer of Twain and Whitman. By the time the error was discovered, it was too late to, as it were, change horses. Now there *is* at least one other Michael King in New Zealand, known as Mike King. He is Maori, a stand-up comic, and several years ago he won the entertainer of the year award, and I received about half of his congratulatory mail. I am *not* a stand-up comedian — though I am, on occasions, a sit-down one. Was there any possibility, I wondered, that Janet had confused us? Had she intended to defuse the painful episodes of her life by having them sublimated as comedy? I checked with her. No, she had not.

Back in Palmerston North in August 1995, we talked of how we might proceed. I believed that, if she were prepared to co-operate with me, to talk with me, to make her papers and her friends and family available to me, that I would need something like two and a half years for research, and a further two years to write a manuscript in close consultation with her. There would then be something like a six-month period in which the book was in production. That added up to about five years. Janet brightened at once and said, "Of course I'll be dead by then." And that thought seemed to make the whole idea not just tolerable, but more acceptable.

As things turned out, that timetable was accurate. The biography is to be published in New Zealand in August of this year, exactly five years since we first discussed it. Janet has been persuaded not to die, and consequently is viewing the imminent prospect of publication with some apprehension. But she has been immensely generous, and immensely courageous, about doing the things we agreed to do.

I spent the bulk of the first year of research interviewing her on and off tape, sometimes as often as two or three times a week. In that same year I went through her papers, which turned out to be voluminous but unorganised. I spent the second year doing other research in New Zealand, the United Kingdom and the United States, and everybody I hoped would talk to me did so, barring two people. And one of those two was the Irishman in London whom she calls Patrick Reilly in the autobiography and who, even though he is an octogenarian, displayed extraordinary cunning and stamina in managing to avoid and outwit me at every turn when I was in London.

There were other anxious moments in the course of overseas research. Barbara Wersba, a gargantuan lady of Russian-Jewish descent, threw open her door on Long Island and bade me in a strong baritone to "Come inside and see my Hairy Willy." "Hairy Willy", to my relief, turned out to be some kind of shaggy terrier, whom Wersba occasionally put on the phone to talk to Janet's cat, Penny. Both women asked me not to put this in the biography. I haven't.

Research in Oamaru turned out to be a fascinating part of the project, for reasons that will be apparent in the book itself. Several members of long-standing Oamaruvian families went out of their way to ask me if I knew that the Frames had what they called "Maori blood", but would never admit it. Well, they never "admitted it" for the simple reason that it was untrue. The rumour originated in a misreading of Janet's story, *The Lagoon*, in which the narrator has a Maori great-grandmother. The whaler Worser Heberley had had two wives, and one of them was Maori; but Janet's family, on her mother's side, were descended from the Pakeha wife.

Another false lead, also communicated to me in whispers, was the story that Janet had an unacknowledged son: inevitably, he had bushy red hair and freckles; and he was, I was told, a regular patient at psychiatric hospitals. This rumour appeared to be a conflation of a misunderstanding of something Janet said in 1974 ("If I'd had a son, he'd be that age now"), and a misguided attempt on the part of a schizophrenia patient to make his case more interesting to those who were treating him. And in that last circumstance there was a chilling echo of Janet's efforts to make her own case more interesting to people such as John Money and the Maudsley Hospital staff.

A source of interest for me was to discover those points of the subject's history that intersected with my own life. I found that, at the very time a physicist named Alan Phillips was taking photographs of me with student friends at Victoria University in the mid-1960s, he was also taking photographs of Janet and courting her. I discovered, too, that Janet had been a fellow passenger on the last voyage of the passenger ferry *Rangitira*, though I hadn't recognised her at the time. And I was disturbed to find that what I had viewed as an errand of mercy in 1982 — rescuing Frank Sargeson's papers from his empty and tinder-dry house while he lay in the geriatric ward of North Shore Hospital — was seen by Janet at the time as an indecent act. "Frank's executor and a historian from Auckland University are even now going through his private papers, as if he were dead," Janet reported disgustedly to a friend in America.

Perhaps the strangest juxtaposition in the course of the whole project occurred the day I accompanied Janet around all the old Frame haunts in Oamaru. As part of this exercise we followed the Janet Frame Heritage Trail, which ended at the site of Willowglen, the Frames' last family home in the town. Here we discovered that the owners of the adjacent property had established an animal park. As we looked at Willowglen, we were in turn watched by a crowd of disconsolate alpacas and wallabies. Janet decided not to climb the hill to see the remains of the house, though she couldn't resist turning to me and quoting, "Wasn't this the site, asked the historian, of the original homestead?" To which, of course, I replied, "Couldn't tell you, said the cowman, I just live here, he said." At that very moment two young adult backpackers emerged out of the undergrowth, having just come down the hill. They walked over to Janet and the man said, "*Do* go up there. If you know anything about Janet Frame, you'll find it absolutely fascinating." They would, of course, have found it even more fascinating if they'd known to whom they were talking. But they didn't, and the moment passed.

Encounters of *that* kind, Janet relished as much as I did, I believe. What she did not enjoy was having to re-live those parts of her life which had caused her pain or grief; and her pet aversion, which I came to call Hunting the Allusion.

In addition to being elusive, Janet was and is a highly *allusive* writer. Her fiction, poetry and autobiographies are an echo chamber of things she has heard or read. And some of her cleverest work parodied the writing of others. When she lived on Waiheke Island, for example, and was disturbed by subdivision activity, she wrote:

> We are the front-end loaders
> we are the movers of earth
> wheel-deep in drainage odours
> assisting at bungalow's birth
> we are the grim foreboders
> of a world without trees or mirth

This, of course, is heavy with the imprint of Arthur O'Shaughessy's Ode, which begins: "We are the music-makers/We are the dreamers of dreams/Wandering by lone sea-breakers/And sitting by desolate streams . . ."

And then, when East Baltimore was razed by fires and riots in 1968, in the wake of Martin Luther King's murder, she wrote to John Money, who was still living there:

> O to be in Baltimore now that April's there,
> for whoever wakes up in Baltimore finds some morning unaware
> that the strongest lock on the five-lock door
> has been smashed (as so many times before)
> and the sweat of fear is on everybody's brow
> - in Baltimore now.

Janet's preference was that such pieces not be quoted; or, if they *were*, that they simply be quoted, without reference to Robert Browning or whoever. Her view was that those who recognised the allusion found their own reward; those who did not, did not deserve to be told. Her wish was that readers and critics simply enjoy eating the pudding instead of putting in their thumb and pulling out a plum, and by so doing announcing what good boys they were. And it was this preference that had made her uncomfortable about the function of literary criticism in general which, she said, produced newly sprung essays "with my own books lying alongside them like shrivelled skins".

By the beginning of 1998 Janet had returned to Dunedin, the city in which she had been born, joking as she did so — although one is never quite sure about this — that she was moving for the benefit of her biographer, to give her life a degree of symmetry that, because of her numerous shifts, it might otherwise lack. I was fortunate to get the Burns Fellowship for that year and for the first six months of 1999, which enabled me to write the biography in that close collaboration which we had agreed upon.

The procedure we adopted was that I would draft two or three chapters, give them to her, leave them with her for about a week while she read and thought about them, and annotated them; and then I would return and we would discuss them. Sometimes I had made errors of fact, which we then corrected; sometimes she *thought* I had made errors of fact, for which I would then produce the evidence; sometimes she decided that some episodes were too raw or intensely private to permit publication, and I would either modify my account of them or remove them.

Wherever another living person was involved in the narrative, I allowed them to see what I proposed to write, and sometimes modified those passages if they had sound suggestions to make.

Does this make the book an "authorised" biography? Not quite. It is a biography written in consultation with its subject, because that is the only way in which it *could* have been written. But it is one in which I as author have made the final decision about what is and is not to be published. It is very much to Janet's credit that she not only consented to reliving, with me, some of the most painful episodes in her life; but she also recognised my right, as a fellow professional, to make final decisions about treatment and content.

Did there turn out to be room for a Frame biography in addition to the autobiography?

Most emphatically yes. Janet Frame's biography is a book from which one learns a great deal about life, and about the business of living, as a result of her extraordinary ability to see and to evoke the nuances of human character and behaviour. It is about her; but it's also about *all* of us and the moral dilemmas we face. In addition, the nearly-four decades of Frame's life since 1963 have been even more eventful than the nearly-three decades that preceded them. Among those who turn out to have walk-on roles in the second half of her life are Iris Murdoch, John Dos

Passos, Philip Roth, William Styron, Bertrand Russell's long-time mistress Constance Malleson, a smattering of Rockefellers and Rothschilds, even the Queen.

It was the very eventfulness of that time, plus the fact that it included relationships with people still living or only recently dead, that impelled Frame to close off the autobiographies where she did. It has been easier for a biographer to deal with those years than it would have been for the autobiographer: because the position of biographer is a more distanced one than that of a participant-observer; and because a biographer, by the very fact that he surveys a far wider range of evidence, is perhaps in a more favourable position than the autobiographer to provide a balancing context.

And that same comment has application to the years covered in the autobiography. Janet Frame, like any other memoirist, wrote from the vantage and viewpoint of her own experience. The biographer casts the net wider and fixes his narrative at the places where many viewpoints and lines of evidence intersect. And, thus rendered, the biographical narrative has contours that are startlingly different in places from the autobiographical story. Similarly there is the fact that the "I" at the centre of autobiography frequently has no idea of the ways in which the decisions and actions of other people contribute to outcomes which impact on the individual. It is the responsibility of the biographer to explore this territory.

Was I confident of my ability to do justice to this subject through the medium of biography? Not always, I would have to say. And it may have been symptomatic of my apprehension that, while writing this book, I began to have recurring dreams about an episode that occurred in my childhood:

I am fishing off the Paremata Boating Club jetty. I have a light line and small tackle, in preparation for catching spotties. But something much bigger takes the bait and begins to pull the line away from me sharply. Instinctively I know not to jerk it, nor even to pull hard against the fish's movement. I let the line out as the fish goes away from me, and haul it in steadily as it comes towards me, keeping it all the while taut. At last, after ten minutes of to-ing and fro-ing, which seems much longer than that, I am able to pull the fish to the surface of the water below me. It is an enormous old-man trevally, the largest I've ever seen.

In my dream, my adult self knows that the only chance of landing it safely is to jump off the jetty into the water, grasp the fish with both hands by the gills and draw it ashore. But my child-self does what I did at the time: tries to haul the fish up and out of the water. And, as soon as the head is above the surface, the body becomes heavier and the whole trace — hook, line, sinker — slides out of the trevally's mouth. The fish, ever so slowly, sinks backwards into the water, rolls over once, then heads back into the deep, receding in size until it disappears.

An analysis of this dream would, I suppose, relate it to my anxiety about whether the medium of biography is too fragile a tackle to bring this particular subject out of the depths and into the light. Or, more worrying, does it suggest that it is my own equipment as a biographer that is too slight for the purpose? Will my subject too, having broken the surface, slip back into the depths and roll away with a flick of her tail? Or is it just a reminder that writerly ambitions amount to a fish that will always get away? I don't know, I don't know. And, of course, as one always does, I await some form of external adjudication.

&

Janet Frame: Antipodean Phoenix in the American Chicken Coop

A paper presented at the American Association of Australian Literary Studies Conference in Florida, 20 April 2001.

JANET FRAME HAS A WORLDWIDE REPUTATION as a New Zealand writer — as the author of twelve novels, four story collections, one collection of poetry and three volumes of autobiography; and, despite her role as a terrestrial manifestation of God's notorious reluctance to be seen, she has frequently been identified as a candidate for the Nobel Prize for Literature — being on the shortlist for that award as recently as three years ago. She does have American associations, however. She spent a significant portion of her career in the United States in the 1960s, 1970s and 1980s, where she met such writers as John Dos Passos, May Sarton, Eudora Welty, Hortense Calisher, Grace Paley, William Styron, Philip Roth, Alfred and Ann Kazin, Granville Hicks, Charles Neider, and John P Marquand Jr.

Frame has also had an American publisher for the past forty-one years: the redoubtable George Braziller of New York. Braziller is wonderfully warm and gentlemanly; but he is one of those publishers who believes that "a good book sells itself", and that consequently promotion is unnecessary. This may have been true at the start of his career, more than sixty years ago. It certainly is true no longer. Hence he has never been able to translate Frame's excellent American reviews into sales of books. Other publishers such as Ben Huebsch of Viking and Sonny Meta of Knopf would have killed to have Frame on their lists. But she has remained faithful to Braziller, because he was interested in publishing her in 1959 when nobody else in the United States was. Whenever her agents urged her to change American publishers, Frame always said, "Not while George is alive". Braziller is still alive and publishing out of Manhattan in his eighty-sixth year.

The story of Frame's first encounter with May Sarton will serve, perhaps, to introduce Frame's American connections. The two writers met in Peterborough, New Hampshire, in November 1969, when Frame was working at the MacDowell colony for writers, artists and musicians. A mutual friend took them out to dinner and Frame, as was her wont, spent much of the evening listening to Sarton, as the older woman talked about her friendship with Leonard and Virginia Woolf, the Huxleys, and other members of the Bloomsbury set that she had known thirty years earlier.

Then, in a change of subject, Sarton began to discuss fan mail. To bring Frame into the conversation, she asked if the New Zealander had ever received letters from admirers. "I did get one once from Patrick White," Frame said in her most tentative voice. Sarton, who had put the question to her in charity rather than in expectation of an impressive reply, asked, "When was this?" "Six years ago," said Frame. "Did you reply?" "Not yet," answered Frame. "Then you must," said Sarton. "All I get is letters from women in basements in Ohio with rats nibbling their feet."

The letter from White had arrived in 1963 when Frame was living and writing in London. No copy has survived, but Frame at the time told Bertrand Russell's former mistress, Constance Malleson, that it was "so wonderful and unselfish, particularly from one writer to another, that I've not been able to answer it." Some clue to what it may have said can be gleaned from White's letters to other people that same year. He told his American publisher, Ben Huebsch, that Frame's work always made him feel "a couple of steps out from where I want to get in my own writing." And to his friends Geoffrey and Ninette Dutton, he speculated that Frame's sojourns in mental hospitals had probably given her "just that extra insight to burrow further than the rest of us".

Frame did eventually reply to White's letter, twenty-two years after she had received it. "When your letter came," she wrote at last, "I was so much overwhelmed that I couldn't think how to answer it. It has now become part of my life . . . as THE letter and has . . . assumed a literary life of its own. As the years passed I found it harder to answer. I'm using the left-over courage needed on a jet flight to Sydney, to greet you [and] to say thank you for your encouragement and for your own wonderful writing . . ."

On this occasion, in November 1985, Frame was visiting Australia for the second time with her niece, Pamela. She had first tried to speak with White. But the by now Nobelled writer declined to come to the phone, citing illness as an excuse. White's biographer, David Marr, gave a different reason for his refusal to communicate, however. White "didn't want to disturb the very detailed fantasy he'd come to have of her . . . as mad, shy etc. It was violation enough of that image that she had crossed the Tasman . . . The vision would have collapsed [altogether] if she'd crossed the threshold and sat down to tea. He didn't want her to be ordinary . . . so he fobbed her off."

One party who did want Frame to be ordinary, and which threatened to reject her when she seemed not to be, was the United States immigration service. In June 1970 Frame had written to May Sarton that she wanted to abandon New Zealand in favour of the United States. "I miss the warmth of my faraway friends," she wrote, "and I am homesick for darkness and burial in snow; I want to do away with the ever open-eyed sun and light [of New Zealand] . . ." She applied for an immigrant visa to the United States as a first step towards seeking residence; and she sent with it glowing testimonials from the writer and critic Charles Neider (who said that Frame "would do us an honour to reside among us") and from the Baltimore sexologist John Money. She also sent a citation from the Mark Twain Society, which had already made her a "Daughter of Mark Twain". (Her honorary membership of the American Academy of Arts and Letters would also have helped, but this was still sixteen years away.)

The whole project collapsed when the immigration service insisted that Frame declare whether or not she had ever been mentally ill or currently suffered from a mental illness. According to New Zealand hospital records, the ones from which the authorities might seek verification, Frame was schizophrenic; and schizophrenia is not a condition from which one recovers. According to her London hospital records, she was not and never had been schizophrenic; but these were not the documents pertinent to her application as a New Zealand citizen. The very fact that this issue was raised at all, along with an interest in whether she was or ever had been a member of the Communist Party, was a considerable shock to Frame. Like children the world over she had learned by heart the wonderful words by Emma Lazarus inscribed on the Statue of Liberty: "Give me your tired, your poor,/Your huddled masses yearning to be free,/ The wretched refuse of your teeming shore,/ Send these, the homeless, tempest-tossed to me." It never occurred to Frame that there might be a proviso: "Send only such wretched refuse as has never been mentally ill or belonged the Communist Party." The episode left such a bad taste that she withdrew her application for an immigrant visa and never again applied for one.

She continued to visit the United States on visitor's visas and to write there, however, especially at the Yaddo Colony in upstate New York, at John Money's house in Baltimore, and at the home of artist friends on the West Coast. She wrote the greater part of three novels there, *Intensive Care*, *Daughter Buffalo* and *Living in the Maniototo*; and her last novel, *The Carpathians*, drew extensively on her American friendships and experience. She also wrote stories and poems and much of her three autobiographies there. She became in due course, as I have mentioned, an honorary member of the American Academy of Arts and Letters, an occasion when, to her great pleasure, she was hosted by John Kenneth Galbraith and embraced by Normal Mailer. Knowing as she did that Mailer had once stabbed one of his wives, Frame was at first fearful when she saw the pugilist writer approach her with a look of determination. But he had nothing more intrusive in view than a kiss, and that she was able to accommodate.

On other occasions Frame wrote limericks about her fellow writers at Yaddo and MacDowell that became famous among other residents there for their ingenuity and saltiness. Let me give you but one example:

> The pecker of Harrison Kinney
> Is so excessively skinny
> That, like a Greek statue,
> His balls stare back at you,
> With little eyes, nosey and chinny.

She also exchanged mildly indecent letters with Philip Roth, of which one of the more mild, from him, delivered to her at Yaddo, read:

> Dear Mrs Breast, It has come to my attention that you have not only failed to pay your rent on the nest we have provided for you, but that you sit there all day twittering your little ass off. Between the twittering and the chirping, the other little birds are having a hell of a time getting their eggs laid. They are a flock of very pissed-off birds, Mrs Breast, and if I were you I'd watch my tail. Yours, Simon Legree.

Philip Roth's third novel, *Portnoy's Complaint*, had just been published at the time he overlapped at Yaddo with Frame. And this juxtaposition impelled Frame's mentor, Frank Sargeson, to write as follows to his friend William Plomer: "When Janet returns to New Zealand, I shall particularly want information from her about whether she was compelled to clean up Roth's mess in the bathroom whenever she was next in the queue."

Frame had, and still has, a lengthy but ambivalent relationship with the Baltimore sexologist, John Money. It was to him that she sent some of the best examples of her parody-poems. When, for example, Money had sent her news of his controversial and therapeutic work with hermaphroditic children:

> Be polite to your hermaphrodite
> Don't beat him when he sexes
> or send him packing out of sight
> to Tennessee or Texas.
>
> A little spark though he may be
> his current surely flows
> directly or alternately
> or maybe both of those.
>
> So interfere not with his fuse
> but watch his wattage flower.
> You never know when you may lose
> your own electric power.

Frame's closest American friend was and is the San Francisco artist

William Theophilus Brown, whose own associations with the likes of Stephen Spender, Igor Stravinsky and Christopher Isherwood, brought another gallery of interesting people into Janet Frame's life. Indeed, it was Isherwood's partner, Don Bachardy, who drew the only really good portrait Frame has ever had done, and which we used on the spine of the American edition of the biography.

For the best part of a decade, too, Frame enjoyed the patronage on the east coast of the writer John Marquand and his wife Sue. Marquand, descendant of the old colonial aristocracy of Newburyport, Massachusetts, dazzled Frame with his good looks, charm and wicked sense of humour, and his interesting associations with the rich and famous — Buckminster Fuller was a cousin; and one of Marquand's aunts was married to John D Rockefeller III.

Marquand himself had courted Jacqueline Bouvier before she became involved with John F Kennedy and, according to one published rumour, had deflowered her in a lift in Paris. Frame stayed with the Marquands in New York, in an apartment that had once belonged to Lionel Barrymore, in Martha's Vineyard, and — most interestingly of all — she spent two Christmases with the family on Salt Cay, a privately owned island in the Bahamas. These latter occasions included an assortment of house guests, among them Rockefeller and Cabot relations, William Styron, who had just won a Pulitzer Prize for *The Confessions of Nat Turner*, and Jason and Barbara Epstein. As usual Frame's view of all this was quirky and inimitably her own.

"Meals," she told John Money by letter, "are at eight, one pm and six thirty, with nothing in between. Have you ever found yourself starving on a coral island, surrounded by ripe coconuts, but without a machete to break them open?" One night she joined the poker school, but had to withdraw when she discovered that the men were not playing with matchsticks but with very large sums of money running into thousands of dollars. She also shared the embarrassment of the whole party when John Marquand's half-brother had to be taken to an asylum in Nassau. Money was required to secure the admission, and all the wealthy people present, in that pre-credit card era, were carrying chequebooks and not cash. The hospital authorities did not recognise them as "people of prestige" and were unimpressed by such names as Rockefeller, Rothschild and Cabot.

To her American friends, Frame was, to quote one of them, novelist and critic Alan Lelchuk, unforgettable with "her frizzy wild hair, her cheeks ruddy . . . [and] her high clear voice, with [its] hometown accent." Lelchuk, who was fourteen years younger than Frame, confessed to an attraction that "grew on me quietly . . . She had a wildness about her, on display, for example, in the evening ping-pong games . . . [and] of course her wild imagination — a Bronte sister resting up in Yaddo."

If, in all of this, I have chosen to refer to Frame as a phoenix rather than as a Bronte sister, it is because of the extent to which she came alive in the United States, even in the immediate wake of stress and grief. Why was this? Partly it was the relief of knowing that she was unlikely to run into strangers who would recognise her and know of her incarceration for the better part of a decade in mental hospitals in New Zealand. Partly too it was because of the joy of recognising America as the home and the location of the earliest poems and novels she had encountered in her childhood and adolescence: the work of John Greenleaf Whittier, Henry Longfellow, Edgar Allan Poe and Hariett Beecher Stowe.

It was also because, in the streets of New York and the slums of East Baltimore, she experienced what she called an acute sense that she was living "in the midst of the human condition" — a sense that was almost always absent from her places of quiet suburban residence in New Zealand.

Most pervasively, however, Frame experienced a feeling of freedom in the United States, which allowed people to be what they chose to be. "[One] can deplore . . . almost everything happening in America," she wrote to her friend Frank Sargeson, "except that apparent ability . . . of people to lead the kind of [intellectual and] moral life they chose." And it was that aura of freedom which she breathed in like oxygen that enabled her to live in the United States with an assertiveness and a panache that she never quite accomplished in New Zealand, her home country.

&

Framing the Founding Fathers: Preposterous Lies about the Canon

An address to open a literature conference at Otago University in March 2000. The conference was dedicated to the doyen of New Zealand literary critics, Lawrence Jones, to mark his retirement from university teaching.

MAY I FIRST MAKE MY OWN TRIBUTE, and congratulate Lawrence Jones, in whose honour this conference has been called. He is, to my mind, the long distance runner of New Zealand literary criticism: both in the sense that he has been doing it, and doing it well, for an extraordinarily long time; and in the sense that he takes no shortcuts — when Lawrence undertakes a topic he does the necessary legwork, meticulously, laboriously, comprehensively, so that you encounter, when you read him, none of those gaps in the argument or dangling questions that can make the work of some other critics so infuriatingly partial and unsettling.

I'm sorry that you'll be largely retiring from teaching, Lawrence. And I offer a lament to the students who may not now encounter you in the flesh, as it were. But I've greatly valued my modest association with you over the previous eighteen months, and the help you gave me with specific investigations. And I look forward to an outpouring of writing that I'm certain will enrich *your* retirement and *our* subsequent reading.

With a virtuosity that I hoped might excite Lawrence's admiration, even, perhaps, the admiration of Patrick Evans had he been here, I chose the title of tonight's opening address to give me the option of going in one of two directions.

If I had completed the biography of Janet Frame at this point, I was going to attempt an analysis of Frame's views of the writing and the lives of Sargeson and Hyde; and assess how they had influenced her *picture* of herself as a writer, and her writing; and, for good measure, throw in, too, her views of Allen Curnow and Denis Glover. Hence "Framing the Founding Fathers".

If I had *not* finished the biography, I proposed to speak on the role of the *authorised* biographer — in this instance the biographer of Frank Sargeson — in policing the reputation of his subject, and attempting to keep views and assessments of that subject within the bounds of verifiable evidence and plausible possibility. Hence reference to "Framing a Founding Father" in another context and another meaning.

I have now to announce to you — or perhaps it is more appropriate to say *confess* to you — that the Frame biography is *not* finished: I am three-quarters of the way through the final chapter. And that, consequently, I am uplifting the second alternative, the role of the authorised biographer in the face of publication of preposterous lies about his subject. And I shall be talking of Frank Sargeson, though my comments have equal application to the "defamation" of other dead famous writers. I place the word "defamation" in inverted commas, because of course it is impossible to defame the dead *legally*; one can do it only morally or metaphorically. And in the case of Frank Sargeson, there is an ample sufficiency of both kinds of example . . .

Can I begin by suggesting to you that *authorised* biographers — and I mean "authorised" by the subject, the subject's family, or the subject's estate — carry a terrible burden. And it is a burden to which unauthorised or debunking biographers are not bound. The authorised biographers are expected by those who authorise them to leap to the defence of their subjects, living or dead, every time somebody else criticises or reviles them. I've borne this responsibility for Te Puea Herangi, Whina Cooper, Peter Fraser and Frank Sargeson; and, no doubt, I'll be expected to bear it for Janet Frame.

One reason one assumes the responsibility, of course, is that the biographer is usually more au fait with the minutiae of the subject's life than are people who are more casual observers; or than critics who might, perhaps, be motivated more by malice than knowledge. Not infrequently pejorative or "defamatory" comments have their origins in ignorance, misunderstanding or an absence of context.

But there are other occasions when the responsibility assumes *you* as biographer; or is *laid* upon you by alert, expectant, even paranoid relatives, executors or trustees. We helped *you*, they are inclined to say in these circumstances; now you are going to acknowledge the existence of that debt by helping *us*. Such instances can be tricky indeed for the biographer, and the implied obligation to help less soundly based than in the previous set of circumstances. Let me give you one example, a non-literary one.

When my biography of Whina Cooper was published in 1983, we waited in some trepidation for the reviews. And when I say "we", I mean the author, the subject (who was still very much alive), and the subject's family. The trepidation was not simply of the ordinary variety that follows book publication. (You know what I mean: have I got it right? Is there some unforgivably elementary error to be picked up and waved around by the reviewer in triumph? Has one been dyslexically unaware of one's own spelling mistakes or misprints?) No, the trepidation was heightened in this case by the fact that a large number of people, mainly Maori, were deeply suspicious of Whina Cooper and were likely to challenge the notion that she was even *worth* a biography, let alone one that gave her credit for some talents and some achievements.

And the inevitable occurred. The morning that the *New Zealand Listener* review of the book appeared, and it is generally the *Listener* reviews which attract most attention and responses, I had a phone call from one of Whina's relatives. "The old lady is outraged. She's never been subjected before to calculated insult by a national publication. What are you going to do about it?" About what? He wouldn't quite tell me over the phone. He just said that when I saw it I would be as angry as he and the family.

I had to wait until my subscription copy of the magazine arrived in that day's mail. And when it did arrive, I saw what had happened. The reviewer of the book, an Auckland Maori academic, referred to Whina as "Te Tema o Tai Tokerau". And this expression was repeated in the headline. And what it was, was a very clever and very calculated insult of a kind favoured in Maori discourse, where a relatively small number of words means that most of them carry multiple meanings. At one level, to call somebody "he Tema" meant simply to call her "a Dame", the word being a simple trans-literation. And Whina Cooper, as a Dame Commander of the Order of the British Empire, quite clearly *was* a dame.

At another level, that same word, tema, was vulgar idiom in Tai Tokerau or Northern Maori dialect for vagina. So the country's leading national magazine had not only called the country's best loved Maori leader, indeed, the Mother of the Nation, a vagina: it had done so in headlines.

What could we do about it? What could the *biographer* do about it? In the end, I had to persuade the family, and Whina herself, that it was best to do nothing. Those "in the know" were the relatively small number of people aware of idiomatic Northern Maori dialect. To make an issue out of it and to demand an apology would have been to let the whole country in on the insult, or the joke — depending on your viewpoint. It would widen the number of people who laughed, and consequently diminish further Whina's mana. It was far better to let that particular sleeping kuri lie.

I might add by way of footnote that Whina did bring that kind of insult upon herself. She had an earthy, peasant-like quality which led her to say and do things that would have appalled Pakeha or church audiences had they been able to understand her. One of her favourite sayings, which she announced on one occasion to a meeting of Maori members of the Catholic Women's League, was that the tactic women in the church should adopt with priests and bishops, to get their way, was to stroke their genitals. She didn't mean it *literally*; she was using a Maori expression that was the equivalent of the English "soft-soaping". But had her words been translated on that occasion for the benefit of the bishops and priests in the audience, she would have caused considerable offence. As it was, all the Maori delegates practically fell off their forms laughing, and the non-Maori-speaking dignitaries simply smiled politely, tolerantly, in ignorance.

Let me now turn my attention to literary examples of a kindred kind.

The first time I found myself called upon to defend Frank Sargeson was some years before I was designated his biographer. I was then merely a humble member of the Frank Sargeson Trust. The trust's fundraising committee's chairman, George Fraser, had died suddenly; and the trust was trying — in the grubby way organisations attempting to raise money for cultural purposes do — to use the *fact* of George's death, and the emotion it aroused, to attract a few more dollars into its coffers. And the purpose of this appeal was to set up the Sargeson Residential Writing Fellowship: to raise sufficient money to convert a set of derelict stables in Albert Park into a writer's studio; and to have enough left over to pay the writer's stipend from investments. Funds would also be devoted to the preservation of Frank's house as a literary museum, a project which, Janet Frame said, would divert time from the study of the Sargeson *novel*, to the study of the Sargeson *hovel*.

It was an uphill battle. George Fraser himself reported going to a corporate board meeting in Auckland to beg for funds, only to be asked: "This Frank Sargeson — did he play for the All Blacks?" George was quick enough to be able to say that he hadn't; but that he went to school with Bert Cook who did — for Cliff Porter's Invincibles, no less.

Anyway, in the wake of George's death, I was invited to an executive meeting of the Auckland Manufacturers' Federation, of which George had been a long-time member and a past president. Was there, the committee asked me, any way they could commemorate George by contributing to our fund? There certainly was, I said, full of unfeigned enthusiasm. I scarcely believed our luck. A ten or a twenty thousand dollar donation would be enough for the Sargeson Trust to close off the appeal and launch the fellowship.

To recognise this contribution, and the fact that it was in memory of George Fraser, the trust would install a plaque in the writer's studio recording the size of the donation and its purpose. And to cap all this off, I had brought with me fifteen copies of the Penguin edition of Sargeson's stories, and I left one copy with each executive member, none of whom had heard of Sargeson previously except as some kind of eccentric friend of George Fraser's. The committee undertook to read the stories, discuss the proposal at their next meeting, and notify the Sargeson Trust of the result.

The upshot was we heard nothing. But the week after my meeting with them, a review of Denys Trussell's biography of Rex Fairburn, written by Antony Alpers, appeared in the *Listener*. (See? The *Listener* again! It figures in an extraordinary number of writers' conspiracy stories.) In this highly discursive piece, Alpers accused Sargeson of being known as someone who "gleefully" procured abortions; and he suggested that this arose from the fact that he was homosexual — if he could not create life himself, then he would take pleasure in destroying it; and he was antagonistic to those who led a healthy heterosexual family life.

This was largely nonsense. As Sir Keith Sinclair wrote in reply, Sargeson knew little about such arcane matters as procuring illegal abortions. The most he would do, and indeed did do on one occasion, was to put a couple seeking an abortion in touch with Irene Lowry, who was *au fait* with such things. As for his supposed hostility to family life, this was vigorously denied by families who related to him as a family: the Finlaysons, the Coles, the Lowrys, the Leaks. The whole set of published comments said far more about Alpers' state of mind and relationship with Sargeson than it did about Sargeson's life.

But the damage was done as far as the Auckland Manufacturers' Federation was concerned. After hearing nothing for four weeks, I contacted the chairman, only to be told that the committee was now exploring some other way to commemorate George Fraser. When I offered to come back to them and answer any questions they might have about Sargeson, he told me with alacrity that they had decided, as an organisation, that they did not want to be associated in any way with Frank Sargeson.

The next little flutter in the Sargeson Trust dovecote occurred the year *after* I had been designated Sargeson's biographer and at the very time I was working on Sargeson's papers at the Alexander Turnbull Library. It was caused by the publication of Patrick Evans' *The Penguin History of NZ Literature*. Examining the career of Robin Hyde, Evans wrote:

"[It] was only when she tried to change her status as a writer, from journalist-amateur to full-timer, that she became in some way a threat to the male writers of the time. Ridicule was one obvious weapon: Sargeson's recollection, for example, turns Hyde into an obsessive figure limping around his bach declaiming her latest work with a string of sausages dangling from her hand. Janet Frame too was to prove a disappointment to Sargeson when they cohabited in the fifties — of both women he recalls, 'One thing I clearly remember about these two women. A spot of housework or cooking was not for them.' The implications are obvious: women should cook for men, not pretend to writing; and what they did write is crazy stuff, odd, expostulatory, hysterical and not to be taken seriously."

I suspect that Evans' general point, about the attitude of male writers to women writers in the thirties, is correct. But in selecting Sargeson as the peg on which to hang his primary accusation, he was choosing a poor target. As I say in the biography, "There was scarcely a man in New Zealand, let alone a writer, who had fewer domestic expectations of women than Frank Sargeson. He prided himself on cooking and caring for his guests, male and female; his complaints were directed against those who did not reciprocate." I could have added that, at the time he was looking after Frame, which included the preparation of all their joint meals, he was also cooking and cleaning house for two ancient aunts in Takapuna and looking after two elderly men friends. In these respects, Sargeson was scarcely a typical New Zealand male, let alone a typical New Zealand male writer of his time.

The Sargeson Trust sent a letter of anguish about this passage to Evans; who quite properly replied that it was all a matter of interpretation. And there that matter rested.

The spectre of Sargeson as a bogey man was raised again, last year, in a *Listener* review of Stuart Murray's book, *Never a Soul at Home*. In that review David Eggleton accused Sargeson of calling Robin Hyde "hysterical", and of "sidelining her prose from his anthology". [*Speaking For Ourselves*] "Her crime was," Eggleton went on to say, "that her kind of writing didn't fit [his] prescriptive categories." Now I should acknowledge here that Eggleton was making a point about both Curnow and Sargeson; and that, in the normal course of things, he is one of the most meticulous, intelligent and readable reviewers we have. But in this instance, in citing Sargeson, he was wrong. *Speaking For Ourselves* was commissioned to showcase contemporary New Zealand story writing. The first qualification of any writer selected for the volume was that he or she be living. Robin Hyde had been dead for six years by the time the book was ready for publication.

As for the comment about "hysteria" — well, that needed to be put into context. As I said in a letter to the *Listener*, for Sargeson, "Hyde's hysteria was apparent in her behaviour rather than her writing. When she lived at Milford and Castor Bay, she frequently interrupted Sargeson late at night and in the early hours of the morning, and on one occasion smashed a window in his company. In these circumstances, 'hysteria' is probably a restrained explanation for what occurred."

Those foregoing comments about Sargeson, by Evans and Eggleton, were of no great consequence. They arose simply from a misinterpretation of evidence or an ignorance of the extent of evidence. There is no suggestion that they were made in bad faith. What is of far greater concern to me, as Sargeson's biographer, and to the Sargeson Trust as the body concerned with maintaining his visibility and protecting his reputation, is the concerted anti-Sargeson campaign that has been waged by a writer who is *not* one of the "sons of Sargeson" — or at least not by choice — Maurice Shadbolt.

In his first volume of memoirs, *One of Ben's*, published in 1993, Shadbolt characterised Sargeson as "a vain, preening and rather paranoid man [who] held court among a mafia of mediocrities". In his second volume, *From the Edge of the Sky*, published this year, he calls Sargeson "vain and petulant, alert to slights, and possessed of a schoolboy's smutty snigger". He refers also to Sargeson's "acolytes, [who] tended to produce just one tidy and tiny book before disappearing".

How to respond to such comments? I feel, as Sargeson's biographer, that I ought to; and I feel that, while there are grains of truth in what Shadbolt says, those grains have been magnified and warped with the passage of time into mountains of distortion.

For a start, who are the "mafia of mediocrities"? Janet Frame? Maurice Gee? C K Stead? Maurice Duggan? Kevin Ireland? Strangely enough two of the writers whom Shadbolt says he admires and respects, Maurice Gee and Dennis McEldowney, are also numbered amongst Sargeson's strongest admirers. The "acolytes who produce just one tidy and tiny book and disappear" could be A P Gaskell, John Reece Cole and Bob Gilbert — but three "failures" out of a dozen or so is not a bad strike rate; and Gaskell's and Cole's books at least were good ones.

What is more difficult to understand is the depth of Shadbolt's dislike of Sargeson himself. It arises from the fact that Shadbolt believes Sargeson dismissed and disparaged his writing and encouraged his "circle" to do the same. Again, there's a grain of truth. Sargeson did criticise some of Shadbolt's early work; and he did encourage Karl Stead to write a pseudonymous letter to the *Listener* about one of them. But that's as far as it went. Shadbolt's view that Sargeson arranged unfavourable reviews of his work in New Zealand and London is wholly unsubstantiated. One of the writers supposedly used by Sargeson in this way, Bill Pearson, was not even speaking to Sargeson at the time and was never an acolyte.

The record of Sargeson's correspondence between 1956 and 1964 tells a very different story from the one Shadbolt writes. In those years, Sargeson sometimes expressed admiration, sometimes reservations, and sometimes exasperation about Shadbolt's potential and performances as a writer. Most often he encouraged his correspondents to read him. Not until after 1965 did Sargeson hold and express the bitterly negative views Shadbolt attributes to him. And he held them from that time because of a review of Sargeson's *Collected Stories* that Shadbolt wrote for the *Bulletin*. And that review is every bit as damning and small-minded as the views Shadbolt says he had to face when he returned to New Zealand from Europe in 1960. Let me quote from it:

"[In] New Zealand Sargeson occupies a place usually reserved for *major* writers elsewhere. At the relatively youthful age of sixty-two, he is now the grand old man of New Zealand letters . . . Wisely [the book's editor] Dr Pearson makes no large claims for the work, and is content to say that Sargeson's example facilitated the development and publication of later New Zealand writers."

The review also spoke of Sargeson's "deadly monotony of style and approach", and said that "his craftsmanship is simply not adequate to the complexity of his subject and theme . . . [That] his talent is in essence minor is evident on comparison with, say . . . Ian Cross and Janet Frame."

The same year that this review appeared, O E Middleton took an action against *Truth* newspaper for libel, and won. One of the documents turned up in that court case was a letter that made it clear that *Truth's* attention had been drawn to the Russian anthology of short stories — that sparked the libel case — by Maurice Shadbolt. Shadbolt denied this before, during and after the case. But the letter was there as part of the court record.

It was the juxtaposition of these two events, the *Bulletin* review and Shadbolt's role in the libel case, that turned Sargeson against the younger writer, and led him to say harsh things about him, in public and in private.

In my view Shadbolt has not only confused the chronology of his account of his relations with Sargeson; he has also confused cause and effect. As to *why* Shadbolt should do this, and remain so adamant about the veracity of his own version, in the face of contrary evidence, I can only note with sadness that he himself has made public announcements that he is being treated for Alzheimers disease.

In these circumstances, is it acceptable to even raise the issue of the accuracy and reliability of Shadbolt's memory and the soundness of his judgment? I can say only that I believe it is: firstly because he con̄ti̇ to write and publish his version of the spat; second̄ intelligent and well informed people, such as Ian Ri̇ the Shadbolt version; and thirdly because Shadbo̅ who has chosen to go public with news of his Alzh̅

I have nothing but sympathy and compassion for the position in which Maurice now finds himself. And I have an enormous admiration for the breadth and depth of his astonishingly large oeuvre of fiction and non-fiction. But as long as he continues to write non-fiction that distorts both recollection and the record, those who have alternative views are, I believe, obliged to present them.

⁘

Is there any quality or condition, apart from the status of authorised biographer, that makes one alert to these kinds of misrepresentations? Possibly a tendency towards pedantry is one. But there is another, I think.

Coming to biography as I do, literary and other kinds, from a background in *history* rather than literary criticism, it is paramount in my view that one establishes, as far as possible, what actually happened before one hypothesises. In other words, I believe one must establish a bedrock of life and times before one launches into an analysis or assessment of the life, the times and the work. Everything one asserts about the *doings* of one's subject must have an evidential base; if it does *not*, then the biographer has an obligation to make this clear.

And so I see the role of the *historian* in literary biography as being not that of the proverbial bull in the china shop, although some of my colleagues might view it that way. It's rather more analogous to the image of Maui trying to toss ropes over the sun and slow its movement across the firmament by anchoring it to earth. In the same way, the historian attempts to tie theoretical luminaries back to evidence and to slow the more fanciful flights of imagination to the point where they can be assessed against demonstrable data. In seeking to do this, of course, the historian also risks the *fate* of Maui, or for that matter of Icarus: that of being scorched by the solar flares of rhetoric more powerful than one's own.

&

On the Purchase of Oysters,
Terakihi and Trollopes

This essay was written for Writing Wellington, Victoria University Press, *a volume commemorating the first twenty years of the Victoria University Writers' Fellowship. It describes the length and depth of the writer's association with the country's capital.*

*I*T WAS JOHN BEAGLEHOLE WHO SPOKE, somewhere, of 'the Regent Street curve of Lambton Quay'. He was lamenting the loss of a harmony of architectural styles that had characterised Wellington's best-known thoroughfare up to the era of gouging and rebuilding that began in the late 1950s.

The comment was pure Beaglehole, apt and felicitous. It arose out of a love for his home city; and it reflected his brand of erudition, and that of his generation of scholars, which viewed so many features of New Zealand life from a perspective conditioned by a thorough knowledge of English history. That same erudition ensured that Beaglehole would have known the identity of Edward Gibbon Wakefield's patron, John Lambton, Lord Durham, for whom the street had been named; and, of course, he was aware of its origin as a genuine quay running alongside the mid-19th century Wellington waterfront, before the uplift of earthquakes and the process of reclamation banished the sea some hundreds of metres to the east. It was the curve of that original beachfront that was responsible for what seemed like a glacier swerve once buildings loomed on both sides of the street.

All of this I now know and understand. In my childhood, however, I had a more elementary view. Then, visiting Lambton Quay was a matter of going to town; and Lambton Quay, I believed, was the whole of that place called 'town'. I have no recollection of venturing beyond it up to the age of nine. There was no need. The Quay contained all the places that, for us, 'going to town' implied. My father's office at the advertising agency Carlton Carruthers du Chateau and King was in the South British Insurance Company Building down the Plimmer Steps end. The Bank of New South Wales, where my father persuaded a senior staff member to put aside Victorian and Edwardian currency for my collection of old coins, stood next door. The booksellers and stationers Whitcombe and Tombs, where we bought family copies of New Zealand classics (Oliver's *New Zealand Birds*, Graham's *A Treasury of New Zealand Fishes*, and Powell's *Native Animals of New Zealand*) was close by.

Right alongside Plimmer Steps was the fish shop run by the Barnao family where, like all good Catholics, we bought seafood on Fridays. This last was the subject of what would now be judged a politically incorrect song that my father would sing on the way home in the car, to the tune of 'O Sole Mio'.

> Bartolo Barnao
> Of Lambton Quay,
> He sella da oyster,
> Da teraki' . . .

This, I found out later, was a variant on a song sung about an even earlier fish shop owner, Nick Fernando.

And there was more. Tony Paino and Vince Criscillo's fruit and vegetable shop, bursting with an unimaginable selection of produce. The man with a basket of flowers down the Woodward Street end who called out, 'Aaa, lovely Otaki violets . . .' The DIC and Kirkcaldie and Stains department stores, where we did Christmas and birthday shopping and were served by immaculately dressed women in black skirts and white blouses. And the Quay was the last domain of that now extinct breed, the street photographer, who took our pictures in a variety of family combinations as we strode along verandah-covered footpaths.

The reason that 'going to town' provided such a sense of occasion, and that all these sights seemed so exotic, was that we lived on the then rural arm of the Pauatahanui inlet, where there was nothing remotely urban or suburban (Cambourne and Whitby were later intrusions). Getting to town, by train or by car, not only involved transporting ourselves to a different landscape; it was very often a different weather system too by the time we emerged from the second train tunnel or from the bottom of the Ngauranga Gorge and saw what Wellington and its colosseum of hills had in store for us. The meteorological transformation often seemed as complete as it would have been were we visiting another country.

My first recollections of the Quay itself are shadowy and generic — just an awareness of being in a canyon of high grey and brown buildings, of trams rattling past down the centre of the road, and of being jostled by the constant movement of pedestrians. There was a touch of fear in that experience, and a need to keep a firm hold on my mother's or my grandmother's hand. But the dominant memory is one of excitement at the sight of so much mobile and noisy humanity. The same set of feelings came back to me when I walked for the first time down Fifth Avenue, which was cavernous and crowded to an extent Lambton Quay never was — but my perspective as an adult in New York in the 1970s matched that of a small child in Wellington in the late 1940s.

My second memory is highly specific. On 15 December 1950, my fifth birthday, fulfilling a promise made one year earlier, my mother and grandmother took me to afternoon tea at Kirkcaldie and Stains. It's not the tea itself I recall vividly, though I do remember the cake-stand, its tiers of plates loaded with miniature sandwiches, scones and cakes on doilies. What I remember with absolute clarity is that we trooped to the window to watch, passing in the street below us, Peter Fraser's funeral cortege.

I knew nothing of bereavements, nor of the rituals and pageantry surrounding death, let alone the death of a wartime prime minister. And so I was intensely interested. The slow procession was led by an armoured personnel carrier hauling a gun carriage. On that carriage lay the coffin, covered with a kiwi-feather cloak, a symbol of leadership whose warm earth colour and soft texture contrasted with the cold steel of the war machine.

Fraser's former colleagues walked in dark suits on either side of the carriage, divided by death as they were in life. The Labour members, who included a family friend, Phil Connolly, were on our side of the Quay. My mother identified them for me as they passed in single file.

Walter Nash out front, now Leader of the Opposition, his square face set in granite solemnity. Behind him Arnold Nordmeyer, whose egglike head was so like the cartoonists' caricatures that he seemed to be imitating them. Then Eruera Tirikatene, tall, silver-haired, handsome in a cloak, not third in party seniority but in that position as chief mourner for the Maori people. Then the rest, unrecognisable and unmemorable to me. By the time they had passed, the government members on the far side, led by the Prime Minister Sid Holland, were too far off to be distinguishable from one another.

Behind the mourners came a line of black limousines. Then lorries loaded with what, at funerals, are always called floral tributes, a blaze of colour in an otherwise sombre sequence. Then an army of trade unionists marching in ranks, shoulder to shoulder. They seemed so soldierlike: not because they were in uniform — on the contrary, they were variously dressed in open-necked shirts and tattered sports coats — but because of their numbers, their formation and, most of all, their grim determination.

All this was watched over by the largest crowd I had ever seen, lining both sides of the Quay, crammed on to shop verandahs, leaning out of windows of buildings such as Kirkcaldie and Stains. Strangely, there was no sound, no audible expression of emotion. The effect was one of solemnity rather than grief — a farewell to a man respected rather than loved. My grandmother, however, who lived then in the railway settlement at Ngaio, dabbed her eyes and announced that he had been a good and great man and a friend to working people.

The years passed. I grew up. Lambton Quay no longer seemed so cavernous at street level. And I learned about other parts of the city: Willis Street, beyond Stewart Dawson's corner, where the handwritten headlines of that day's *Evening Post* were displayed in the street-level window; Manners Street, home of the left-wing bookshop Modern Books; Mercer Street, where Dick Reynolds presided over that marvellous second-hand emporium, Smith's Bookshop; Courtenay Place, with the best of the cinemas and Chinese restaurants; and Boulcott Street, with St Mary of the Angels, where we attended midnight mass at Christmas and Easter and revelled in the sound of Maxwell Fernie's choir.

In every sense that mattered, however, Lambton Quay was still 'town'. In the course of my rare visits to the city from boarding school in the Hutt Valley, my mother would meet me at the railway station. From there, to allow me to experience something called 'coffee bar culture', whose major features seemed to be candles in Chianti bottles and heavily mascara'd women in bouffant hair-dos and fishnet stockings, she would take me to the Rendez-Vous coffee shop near the entrance to Cable Car Lane. (It was a *sine qua non* that such establishments had to have French names: there was also the Chez Paree and the Monde Marie; even the one that did not was still called The French Maid.) On one such occasion at the Rendez-Vous, told that the premises had a newly opened upstairs gallery, my mother led me with our cups and coffee and plates of cream cakes into the adjacent and plush office of a prominent accountant, who was just as startled to see us as we were to encounter him.

Later still, when I was a university student in the mid-sixties, I always took the Kelburn cable car to and from town, so that Lambton Quay was invariably my point of access and egress. It was in these years that I began to haunt Roy Parsons' sparsely elegant bookshop, by this time established in the Ernst Plischke-designed Massey House. An additional enticement there was the coffee bar that Harry Seresin and his mother had opened on the mezzanine floor, which, among many other attractions, was the first Wellington eatery to make and sell yoghurt. Further along the Quay were the Parsons' shabby but enticing bookseller neighbours, Ferguson and Osborne. The business was run by the eccentric and bad-tempered siblings Harold and Vera Osborne, who seemed to have an inexhaustible supply of unopened first editions selling at their original, pre-inflation prices, and who, right to the end, parcelled all purchases in brown paper tied with string.

In those years too I evolved a routine of Friday night drinking. In the case of the crowd I had fallen in with, this meant heading for the first-floor lounge bar of the Midland Hotel. From that genteel den of iniquity other rites of passage followed: the courtship of members of the fairer sex who joined us there, or floated provocatively on our periphery (of the latter, I recall in particular a pair of blonde Dutch-Jewish twins, with plunging necklines and Stars of David on silver chains); the purchase and subsequent juggling of bottles to have in hand for whatever entertainment would complete the evening; the post six-o'clock meals at the steak bar over the road whose name I no longer recall; and the subsequent converging on taxi ranks for transport to the scene of that night's party in Kelburn, Wadestown or Tinakori Road.

Memories of later years speed up, the way recollections do as they approach the present, and are less vivid. In my journalism days, after the abolition of six o'clock closing, there were regular drinking sessions with journalists at Barrett's Hotel (primarily *Evening Post* staffers — Keith Gunn, Doug McNeil, Donald McDonald). And there was an entirely different school at De Brett's made up of the city's Maori professionals (Koro Dewes, Waka Vercoe, Ross White). The writers Alistair Campbell and Harry Orsman gathered for a time with musicians at the Dungeon Bar of the Royal Tavern, then abandoned it for some pub in Willis Street. Twenty years earlier, my father had drunk with Denis Glover, Jim Baxter, Tony Vogt and Lou Johnson in the old Royal Hotel on the same site.

In the early 1970s there was the welcome appearance on Plimmer Steps of John Quilter's bookshop, eventually to shift down to the Quay proper. It was in the original location that I overheard the kind of conversation one dines out on for years afterwards. A flushed gentleman in tweeds burst into the shop and hurtled to the counter, where he asked in a loud voice, "I say, do you have any Trollopes?" There was a silence while the proprietor considered the implications of the question. Then a customer intervened. "Wrong place, mate," he said. "You want Vivian Street."

In 1980 I turned my back on the Wellington district in favour of the winterless north and have made only sporadic return visits. When I *am* back, I am frequently surprised at ways in which Lambton Quay has improved: the pavement cafes, the renovations of such treasures as the Public Trust Building, the extent to which even the buildings which John Beaglehole regarded as intrusions now look as if they belong. I am grateful too for landmarks and reference points that survive, like Parsons' and Quilter's. But I am also aware of the 'silences between' — the businesses and buildings that have entirely disappeared along with the trams: Ferguson and Osborne, the Cadeau giftshop, the Rendez-Vous, the Midland, De Brett's, Barrett's. The Quay is simultaneously familiar and unfamiliar to me as it sheds old skins and acquires new ones.

In one important respect it doesn't change, however. If I ever want to recapture the feeling of belonging to a town, of casting off anonymity, I do it there. In ten minutes at Bowen Street corner, or at the bottom of

Woodward Street, I can be sure of sighting and talking to at least half-a-dozen people I know: old school friends, acquaintances from university, current and retired journalists, civil servants, politicians. Lambton Quay is not, was not and never will be my place of residence. But it brings me as near as I shall ever come in my life to feeling part of an urban community; and it connects my past to my present.

&

Something Nobody Counted On

Published in the Listener, *on 28 April 2001.*

"**F**OR YOU," MY WIFE SAID, passing the telephone. "A Hollywood director." For most writers, even ones living in the United States (which, at the time, we were), ninety-nine such calls out of a hundred turn out to be hoaxes or wrong numbers. But this was neither. It *was* a Hollywood director. I had heard of him. And it was me he wanted.

"I believe you've got a story to tell," he said. Hmm. . . . This required careful handling. I hadn't a clue what he was talking about. "I sure have," I said cautiously, "which particular aspect of it interests you?" "John Cyprian Phipps Williams," he said. Ah. . . . Now all was clear. Somebody had noticed. And he was right. I *did* have a story to tell; or, more accurately, therein lay a story *waiting* to be told. It wasn't *mine*, exactly, I had simply stumbled upon it — or into it.

It had been a source of perplexity to me that in the course of the extensive media promotion I had done for *Wrestling With the Angel*, the biography of Janet Frame, not one journalist had asked me about John Williams. Williams, known to his New Zealand friends as "Jack", had been a brilliant New Zealand cardiac researcher and heart surgeon, a colleague of Brian Barratt-Boyes and other Greenlane Hospital stars.

Most importantly, he had achieved a worldwide reputation in 1961 for his discovery and definition of what came to be called Williams Syndrome. This, like Down's Syndrome, is a chromosomal abnormality which causes children to be born with physical and mental defects; but also with an endearing pixie-like appearance and what has been called a "cocktail party personality" — richly expressive story-telling skills. John Williams also worked in the United States for NASA on the Apollo space programme (investigating the effects of weightlessness on the cardio-vascular system), and for University College, London.

Then, in 1969, after the writer Janet Frame turned down his proposal of marriage, John Williams walked out of his London flat and vanished. His friends and family assumed that he had either been murdered or committed suicide. The rumour mill suggested that his disappearance may have been connected to the "classified" work he had been doing for NASA. Perhaps he had been kidnapped by a foreign power? Or defected? Whatever had happened, nobody in New Zealand, including his family, heard of him or from him for thirty years.

And then, just before the Frame biography went to press, I discovered that Williams was alive and living in hiding in Europe. He was distressed to learn that he was to feature in the Janet Frame book, and he sent a message to me asking that his name be omitted. This presented me with considerable problems. All the information about him which I had included in the narrative came from sources other than Williams himself. The book was typeset and at page proof stage. Publishers in four countries were waiting to print and publish according to long-fixed schedules.

So I sent a letter to Williams via an intermediary, explained my difficulties, and enclosed a copy of what I proposed to publish about him. I said that I would be prepared to consider any alterations to the text that he might propose, even to consider withdrawing him from the narrative altogether if he was able to help me understand his reasons for seeking continuing anonymity. I heard nothing further. And so the book was published with my original references to Williams intact. To the best of my knowledge, he remains in hiding in Europe.

This fact, that he turns out to be alive, is a matter of enormous interest and concern to his surviving friends, to his family (he has a nephew in Wellington who has not seen him since childhood), and to thousands of Williams Syndrome support organisation members around the world. Representatives of all three groups contacted me after publication of the Frame biography and asked for further information. And it was as a consequence of the Williams Syndrome connection that I took the telephone call from Los Angeles.

The director plans to make a film about Williams Syndrome children and their families; and about the gentle and charismatic man who recognised their problem and suggested ways in which they might cope with it. The fact that this man has since disappeared, but survives somewhere in hiding, is regarded as "an integral part of the story's appeal", the director told me. Another appeal, to actors, was the nature of Williams Syndrome. "Hollywood stars love to play handicapped roles," he assured me, "because they invariably lead to Academy Award nominations."

There was one immediate obstacle to his objective, however. As we spoke, the American actors' and screenwriters' guilds were on strike as part of their cycle of contract renewals. All new work had come to a halt. There was no way of knowing how long the impasse would continue. Until it *was* resolved, the director expected to make no immediate progress on the screenplay and casting for the movie.

In the course of researching the Janet Frame biography I had turned up sufficient information about John Williams to be intrigued by the man. He was born in Wellington in 1922 to a shabbily genteel clan which had known better days, materially and socially. His immediate family — parents, Williams himself, a brother and a sister — had lived with a wealthy great-aunt in Abel Smith Street. The implied arrangement was that she would leave her considerable fortune to her relations when she died. She did not, however. She left it to the Presbyterian Church.

Jack Williams, a brilliant student, was educated at his great-aunt's expense. He breezed through science and arts degrees at Victoria and Otago Universities; and then Bachelors of Medicine and Chemistry in Sydney. He was also, in the 1940s, a prominent member of the peace movement and it was in that context that he had met Frank Sargeson's friend Elizabeth Pudsey Dawson, who would later put Williams in touch with Janet Frame.

After graduating with his medical degree in 1953, he spent two years as a house surgeon at Auckland Hospital, a year at Thames Hospital, then joined Brian Barratt-Boyes' cardiac team at Greenlane for seven years, 1956-1962. It was at Greenlane that he noticed that many children admitted for heart surgery shared other characteristics: they had similar facial features; they were chatty and outgoing, especially with adults;

many of them were musically gifted; and yet they also displayed degrees of mental retardation.

Williams speculated that the common features might indicate a syndrome. He was given approval to investigate the condition; and he established that it was caused by "a micro-deletion of part of chromosome 7, which includes the Elastin Gene". This discovery, announced in medical literature in 1961, made an enormous difference to the lives of families with Williams Syndrome children (one in 25,000 of the general population). Diagnosis permitted a better understanding of behavioural difficulties associated with the syndrome and development of strategies to deal with them, where previously there had been none.

It may have been the recognition of the importance of this breakthrough that led to Williams' employment by the Mayo Clinic in Minnesota from 1962 to 1965, on classified work for NASA. He rapidly became disillusioned with this project, however. He told friends that he was working twenty hours a day and not sleeping when he had the opportunity. He feared that he might be heading for a breakdown. The result was that he abandoned the clinic in favour of cardiac research at the department of Physiology, University College, London.

Williams was working in London when he met Janet Frame in August 1967. They were introduced as a consequence of their mutual friendship with E P Dawson, who had by this time moved back to England from New Zealand. Williams offered Frame sanctuary in his flat in St Pancras when she needed a period of convalescence to recover from meningitis. Frame stayed with him for seven weeks and, with their shared interests in literature, music and the theatre, these two normally shy people enjoyed each other's company.

Two years later Frame stayed with Williams at St Pancras again, and again they discovered a pleasant harmony together. Then Williams proposed to her ("Why don't we make it legal?"). Frame was devastated. She had not expected this and did not want it. She took fright and fled to E P Dawson's cottage in Norfolk. When she returned to the St Pancras flat a fortnight later, there was no sign of Williams.

Frame assumed that her friend had left early for a planned holiday in Greece. But Williams was never seen again by his family, nor by his friends in London and New Zealand. Frame never received another communication from him. His brother and sister, alarmed for his wellbeing, asked Interpol to try to find him. That agency found evidence that Williams may have made his way to Salzburg in Austria. But there the scent went cold. Others who knew him *thought* they had spotted him in Bern and Geneva — but these sightings were never confirmed. His brother and sister died without knowing what had become of him.

And there matters rested for the better part of three decades. Janet Frame assumed that her friend was dead — she found it difficult to believe that somebody could know her well enough to propose to her and then never communicate with her again — and so did I as I researched and wrote her biography. Then, towards the end of that project, two proverbial bombshells went off. I discovered that Williams had renewed his New Zealand passport in Geneva, ten years after his "disappearance". And I learned in January 2000, when the Frame book was typeset, that Williams had communicated with a mutual friend by email.

It was in the wake of this second revelation that I attempted to communicate with John Williams, sending him copies of relevant sections of the book and asking for his comments. I received no direct response to this request, however, just a single email message relayed through the intermediary (which may have been sent before he received pages of my text): "I do not wish to be discussed in the book, nor to be the subject of his footnotes, nor to be discussed by Janet Frame. I have strenuously preserved her privacy . . . and ask that I be allowed the same privilege."

With the book about to be printed, with information in it from sources other than John Williams, and with no explanation from him as to why he required complete anonymity, I felt unable to comply with his request. He was, after all, one of only two men to propose to Janet Frame. It was unthinkable that an authorised biography of her life should omit any mention of him, particularly in association with events that occurred more than thirty years ago.

I said, in my letter to John Williams: "I apologise for the fact that it is only now that I am able to be in communication with you. But you will appreciate that it is you who have covered your tracks and made such communication difficult. Let me also say how delighted I am that rumours of your death prove to be exaggerations." I heard nothing further from him.

In the United States this year, I made one further attempt to seek information about Williams' work for the Apollo programme. When I had contacted the Mayo Clinic by telephone in 1998, the person I spoke to was most helpful and confirmed that Williams had worked there from

1 October 1962 to 30 September 1965. If I wanted further information, she said, I simply had to make a formal request in writing.

In March of this year I made that formal request, citing my previous communication with the clinic. This time, the letter in response said: "[The] situation you describe sounds intriguing, and we would like to be of help to you. However, we are unable to provide more than confirmation of [Dr Williams'] employment at Mayo Clinic." Which leads me to suspect that they know John Williams is alive, and that he has asked the clinic, as he is entitled to do, that they release no more information about him.

And there, for now, the matter rests again. I, for one, will not pursue Dr Williams further. I await with trepidation his possible appearance on the Big Screen. And I would, if I could, apologise to him for contributing to that possibility. I would also say to him, however, that such an outcome is made *more* likely by the very mystery which he himself has created and perpetuated; as J D Salinger, Thomas Pynchon and Janet Frame have discovered, the surest way to draw attention to oneself is to make strenuous efforts to avoid the spotlight. As Allen Curnow warned, in a poem John Williams is well aware of, the result of such strategies will always be

> something different, something
> Nobody counted on.

&

The Strange Story of
Reuel Anson Lochore

A memoir of Reuel Lochore, written for Metro, March 1991, *after Wellington businessman Fred Turnovsky had alleged that Lochore had been a Nazi.*

THREE OR FOUR TIMES A YEAR I make the half-hour drive from Auckland to the Whangaparaoa Peninsula. It is a melancholy expedition: not because of the parched landscape between Okura and Silverdale, though that is not much to my liking, nor because of the prefabricated suburbs that have rolled out like a carpet along the so-called Hibiscus Coast. The journey is dismal because I go to see a friend who no longer recognises me, whose personality is dead.

Dr Reuel Lochore is a patient in the North Haven Continuing Care Hospital. At eighty-eight, he is a shrunken caricature of his former self. His head lolls, his eyes roll, he has difficulty talking. When he does speak, his words make little sense. His skin has taken on the parchment quality that comes with illness or old age. His skeletal body can scarcely support its own weight. Any memories he once shared with others have escaped beyond recall. His heart beats strongly, however, denying him release from the kind of senility all healthy people dread.

Reuel Lochore is unaware of his condition, just as he is unaware of the identity of family and friends who call on him. He enjoys eating, drinking and being made comfortable. He enjoys companionship. One visitor, a cousin, just sits silently alongside his bed, and he likes that.

This is the reason I continue to come. This and the fact that nearly twenty years earlier this man and his wife made me welcome in their home only a few minutes' drive from where he now lies. For more than a decade they gave me hospitality, personal warmth and professional encouragement. I became close to them. I grew immensely fond of them.

☞

Reuel Lochore had retired from the New Zealand Diplomatic Service in 1969, after two years as Ambassador to West Germany. He and his wife, the pianist Dorothy Davies, moved into a house on a cliff above Red Beach which commands a stunning view of the northern Hauraki Gulf. There they pursued active retirement. Reuel gardened, was busy in the Auckland German Society and the Institute of International Affairs, and researched and wrote erudite manuscripts on philology and the origins of culture in South-East Asia. Dorothy played and taught the piano and emerged periodically, even in her eighties, to give concerts and master classes in other parts of the country and in Australia.

When I met them in the early 1970s they seemed as contented as any gifted couple could be at that time of life, enjoying the things they could do and resigned about those they could not. She was Dorothy, he was 'Dozo'. Reuel got up early and made startlingly strong coffee before heading to his desk for several hours' work. She read in bed wearing a visor of the kind that journalists used to sport in American movies. They breakfasted together — fruit and toast and more coffee — then fed bread to the sparrows and seagulls that congregated knowingly on the seaward balcony. A colony of pukekos came to the door for their share of scraps. Then they got on with their respective days, meeting for lunch and dinner.

I merged into this routine when I stayed with them. I slept and worked in the downstairs flat and joined them for meals. I had marvellous conversations with Dorothy, who was forever seeing things that nobody else noticed and offering dotty advice. Once, she swore, she had watched two satellites in the night sky approach each other from different directions, meet, then move off together on an entirely different orbit.

"If you get married again," she advised me sternly, "get yourself an older woman. That works much better. And you don't have to worry about all that sex business." She was three years older than Reuel. They had married when he was thirty-six and she forty. They adopted a son, Mark.

In the mid-afternoons I'd stop writing, swim off the beach below, then sit in Dorothy's curtained studio while she practised the piano for several hours: Beethoven sonatas, Bach, Rachmaninov, Schubert. She had studied at the Sydney Conservatorium of Music with Alfred Hill in the 1920s, then at the Royal College of Music in London. This had led to a close association with the Austrian-Jewish pianist Artur Schnabel, with whom she then worked in Italy. Like her mentor, Dorothy became an authority on Beethoven interpretation and performance.

With Reuel, the conversation tended to be about history, prehistory, religion and politics, and often had the quality of a tutorial. His own university work, in New Zealand and Germany, had been an exotic and quixotic mix of languages, sociology and philosophy. He was encyclopaedically knowledgeable and the house was crammed with books on topics that interested him. It was full too of South-East Asian art, especially pieces of Khmer sculpture collected in the course of his diplomatic career.

In his seventies and eighties he still took an almost adolescent delight in discovery and discussion. Who are we? What are we? Why are we here? How could communities better organise themselves to empower individuals to lead more fulfilling lives? He was erudite about Eastern and Western thought systems, how they might have evolved and how they might be reconciled.

I remember his lamenting the fact that, worldwide, universities were training more and more people in more fields than ever before. "If only Goethe were alive to sum it up for us," he said. "It's keeping the score that's so difficult — though not as difficult as the specialists would have us believe." That was Reuel. Interested primarily in the life of the mind and spirit. And forever trying to "keep the score".

My recollection of those years is of a series of hot, clear days, filled in succession with writing, swimming, conversation and music. It was a small taste of the kinds of communities that artists have set up from time to time in Europe and North America. In the late 1970s Reuel and I spent even more time together, working on my biography of Andreas Reischek, for which he deciphered and translated Reischek's, Hochstetter's and von Haast's letters from German Gothic script.

His willingness to do this for nothing, and at the expense of his own work, was entirely typical. He and Dorothy spent considerable time helping people, driving them about, giving them meals and beds, contributing money to worthy causes.

There was a shadow over these good days, however, and it grew steadily larger. Reuel began to fall out with people at an alarming rate; and some of his oddities began to lurch alarmingly towards lunacy. To understand how this occurred, it is necessary to trace the course of his brilliant but erratic career.

Reuel Anson Lochore, son of a Methodist minister and a teacher of the deaf, was born in Stratford, Taranaki, in 1903. His father's family was characterised by intelligence, a strong will to achieve and unabashed eccentricity. The Reverend Jack Lochore had been one of eleven children born on the West Coast goldfields. He had worked as a journalist before opting for theological college.

Later descendants of the clan have included an All Black captain, the founder of a well known real estate firm, an international president of Soroptimists, and the former *New Zealand Herald* journalist and film critic, D W Lochore. Reuel's first cousins through his mother were the famous Alleys: Rewi, Gwen, Geoff, Pip and Joy, all of whom distinguished themselves in their fields. Reuel was especially close to Rewi and corresponded with him for much of his life.

The immediate family moved around New Zealand in response to the Rev Jack Lochore's calling: from Stratford to Christchurch, to Gisborne, Oamaru, Auckland, Petone and Dunedin. From Oamaru, Reuel was enrolled at Waitaki Boys' High School, then under the sway of its charismatic rector, Frank Milner. He thrived there. He responded with enthusiasm to Milner's educational precepts, his British imperialist fervour, and to the rector's conviction that Waitaki boys should take a world view and place their gifts at the service of mankind.

He was an outstanding student and debater and dux of the college in his final year, 1920. That same year, Reuel Lochore brought further distinction to Waitaki by winning the Earl Meath Cup for an Empire-wide essay competition. His subject was *In Praise of Empire*, a literary valuation of patriotic prose and verse from the Elizabethans to the present. The new Governor-General, the Earl of Jellicoe, made a special trip to Oamaru to present the trophy. There were two features of this award that made it an anticipation of Lochore's life to come. One was the confident manner in which the essay had tackled and knocked into shape a subject of cosmic proportions; the other a bizarre error in newspaper reporting of his success. The Press Association at first announced that Reuel had won the cup for small bore rifle shooting — an eventuality that his later companions in the Home Guard would know was utterly unlikely.

After a holiday job with the *New Zealand Herald*, Lochore entered Auckland University College on a Junior National Scholarship to study English, French, Latin, philosophy and psychology. He secured first class passes in all these. His BA was awarded in 1923 along with the Tinline Scholarship for distinction in English language and literature. Three years on he had an MA with first class honours in French and decided to be a schoolmaster in the Milner mould. He joined Wellesley College in Wellington in 1927, where his colleagues included E H McCormick and Bill Mitchell.

In 1930, depressed about the premature death of a close male friend and overburdened by the requirement that Wellesley staff teach cramming classes in the evening in addition to their daytime programme, Lochore headed for Europe to further his studies in language, literature and philosophy. He enrolled successively in the Institut fur Auslander in Berlin, Berlin University, the Institut der Volkerpadagogik in Mainz, and finally the University of Bonn. He emerged in 1935 with *a summa cum laude* doctorate on the history of civilisation, credits in sociology, further experience of philosophy and philology, and fluent in German. He emerged also with a profound admiration for the philosophy, literature and music of the German people. Of which more later.

Back in New Zealand in 1936 Lochore had hopes of a high post in government service. He had arrived home with flattering references from his German supervisors and from Harry Drew, an official at New Zealand House in London who had commended him to Finance Minister Gordon Coates. He had been entrusted also with a "secret mission": a proposal from senior members of the German administration for the consideration of the New Zealand Government. Of this too, more anon.

The government job failed to materialise. And so, after a spell stumping the country and speaking generally favourably about conditions in Germany to whomsoever would listen, Lochore fell back into school teaching. He also joined the Labour Party and became a subscriber and (on two occasions) a contributor to the left-wing journal *Tomorrow*. It was while he was on the staff of Scots College in Wellington in 1938 that he helped organise the visit to New Zealand of the German World War One hero Felix von Luckner — regarded by some members of the Labour movement as an emissary for Hitler's Germany.

In the late 1930s Lochore met the pianist Dorothy Davies, who had returned from study abroad and was staying with the wife of his cousin Geoff Alley. They were drawn together by their affinity for Europe and, in particular, for German music. They married in 1940 and lived first at Hataitai, next to the Alleys, before moving out to the then rural community of Porirua.

Lochore's break into government work was achieved in 1939. As a consequence of his linguistic facility and his acquaintance with Eric McCormick, editor of the Department of Internal Affairs' centennial publications, Reuel Lochore landed the highly secretive job of officer in charge of aliens. Throughout World War Two he was responsible for the surveillance of non-British immigrants, especially those who came from parts of Europe under fascist domination. He read their mail, commissioned reports on their social and cultural gatherings and interviewed those applying for New Zealand citizenship. He also worked with the police to check out the hundreds of reports of alleged fifth column activities that came in from throughout the country.

At the end of the war he was able to say that, contrary to the general public perception, the number of aliens supportive of the fascist cause had been infinitesimal. Most immigrants with whom he came into contact at this time saw him as an ally, as someone who shared their love of European culture and whose investigations would establish their bona fides in the eyes of New Zealand officialdom. Some became friends of his and Dorothy's for the rest of their lives. A minority, including Fred Turnovsky, deeply resented being under scrutiny and suspicion, however, and likened Lochore's professional activities to those of the regimes in Europe from which they had fled.

Lochore carried on with his study of languages. By 1946 he was fluent in German, French and Italian, and had a reading knowledge of Dutch, Swedish, Polish, Russian "and most other European languages". He later learned Malay and Sanskrit and developed a reading knowledge of Maori and other Polynesian dialects. From 1946 to 1949 he was the country's naturalisation officer and "Government Translator".

His career took a new direction in 1949. On the strength of what was viewed as his successful work with aliens (and it is worth noting that alleged war criminals recently said to have reached New Zealand were all admitted *after* the term of Lochore's responsibility for refugees), Lochore was made officer in charge of security in the Prime Minister's Department. This entailed the vetting and surveillance of all members of that department and its sensitive twin, External Affairs, and other government agencies. These activities contributed to the sacking of at least one New Zealand diplomat, the forced resignation of two more, and inconclusive suspicion being drawn to others who subsequently completed their careers. Lochore reported primarily to the department's deputy head, Foss Shanahan, sometimes to Shanahan's boss, Alister McIntosh, and occasionally to the Prime Minister himself, Sid Holland.

It was while he was a member of the Prime Minister's Department, in 1951, that Reeds and the Institute of International Affairs co-published a manuscript Lochore had written in 1946. Called *From Europe To New Zealand, An Account Of Our Continental European Settlers*, it used evidence and conclusions he had generated in the course of his wartime work.

According to the conventions of the 1990s the book is ethnocentric, even racist. It claims, for example, that refugees "lack discretion and tact. They revel in displays of emotionalism and self-pity, and fail to realise how we despise such lack of self-control. On social occasions . . . they talk loudly and untiringly about their own affairs. Being bad listeners, they cannot take a hint, nor sense an attitude from what we prefer to leave unsaid . . . If refugees are unpopular, it is no doubt partly because their success has aroused jealousy, but it is in far greater measure because so many of them in a very literal sense do not know how to behave themselves."

Strange as it seems by today's standards, the book was viewed at the time of publication as a plea for tolerance and cultural diversity. It was reviewed widely and there were no unfavourable notices. Even Central and Eastern European immigrants who might reasonably have taken issue with some of its more sweeping generalisations did not do so in print. Harry Benda, a Czechoslovak lecturer in political science, said the book answered "those few but persistent critics who poison the air by constant vilification against anyone with a foreign accent". Lochore, he said, presented immigrants "truly and honestly, as a bunch of different people, some good, some bad, and most of us neither better nor worse than most native-born New Zealanders."

In 1956 Reuel Lochore suffered the first major setback of his later career and one that was to gnaw at him for the next three decades. His recommendations for the setting up of the Security Intelligence Service were not adopted in the form in which he presented them to Sid Holland and cabinet (he wanted a non-military agency staffed entirely by New Zealand public servants and headed by himself). Instead, the service was established on lines proposed by the head of MI5, Sir Roger Hollis, included several former British security agents selected by Hollis, and was headed by Brigadier Bill Gilbert. Lochore believed subsequently that this had allowed Hollis, suspected of being a KGB agent, to place Soviet moles in the senior ranks of the New Zealand security system. He came to believe also that a senior New Zealand civil servant had engineered this outcome.

As a consolation prize, Alister McIntosh offered him a role in the expanding Diplomatic Service, and Lochore rapidly became one of the department's experts on Asia. He served successively in Bangkok, Singapore, Kuala Lumpur, Delhi, Jakarta, and finally Bonn. In all the Asian posts he made a feature of studying local languages and cultures, learning about flora and fauna, and eating local food. He strongly opposed the notion that New Zealanders should follow the British example of living in enclaves in foreign cities.

He became increasingly anti-British, in fact, as his diplomatic career progressed. He tried hard — and largely unsuccessfully — to persuade New Zealand governments to import more manufactured goods from Asia in preference to Britain. And, while he was acting high commissioner in Singapore, he wrote of his British counterparts: "In their social life they seem to be trying to maintain a superiority that they have had to abandon in commerce and politics . . . Most of them are innocent of culture of any sort, let alone Chinese or Malay culture."

While South-East Asia had by this time become the focus of his research activities, Germany remained his major interest and — after New Zealand — his first love. He had lobbied the department for years to establish a German trade and diplomatic post. By the mid-1960s, with British membership of the European Community imminent, the proposal made sense and the government agreed. With his knowledge of the country and its language, Reuel Lochore was the obvious person to establish the mission.

Before he left Jakarta, however, where he was New Zealand Minister, Lochore created a week of panic in Wellington. After McIntosh had informed him of his impending appointment to Bonn, Lochore sent back a cable in Maori. Translated, it read: "The red hand is uppermost. The trees of Tamahae are laughing." McIntosh was perplexed. He assumed that the message referred to the threat of a communist coup in Jakarta, and that it had been sent in Maori to prevent the Indonesians deciphering it. But precisely what it was trying to convey, neither McIntosh nor his advisers could be sure. Pressed for clarification, Lochore revealed that it had simply been his playful way of saying, with reference to the Bonn decision, "Well done, chief, we're all applauding."

Lochore was to spend over two years in West Germany and he was praised by McIntosh and New Zealand cabinet ministers for the manner in which he handled the appointment. He made a considered effort to get beyond gossip and newspaper speculation in his appraisal of European politics and economic strategies, and his long dispatches to Wellington relied more on what he regarded as his skills in sociology and cultural analysis than on the cocktail party circuit.

Much of his time was taken up with the logistics of simply establishing the embassy. He worked hard in a largely unsuccessful effort to increase German tourism to New Zealand and bilateral cultural relations. As he had done in other posts, he accepted a wide range of invitations to speak on erudite topics — a facility which won him applause from the local cultural mandarins.

Dorothy too made a contribution: by giving piano and lieder house concerts, and by being an uninhibited conversationalist at embassy functions (one New Zealander was shocked to hear her tell a confused European diplomat that her country was so egalitarian that, on holiday, "the Prime Minister used to empty his dunny next to us emptying ours"). An ambassador from an Arab country was so smitten with her that, for several weeks, he sent her packets of dates every day.

Some of Lochore's staff found him difficult to work with, however. He exhibited a degree of fussiness, worrying interminably over such issues as whether to follow the British naval system or the orthodox French protocol for seating guests at table. More alarmingly, he seemed unwilling to promote the case for increased lamb and butter quotas in Europe. His attitude was that the Germans had pulled themselves up by the bootstraps after the war and that they would respect New Zealand more if she tried to do the same. He even went so far as to claim that a New Zealand campaign for increased access to the German market would drive local farmers to support the neo-Nazi right wing.

When Lochore reached the mandatory retiring age in 1968, there was no enthusiasm in Wellington for the suggestion that his appointment be extended. He argued with George Laking (McIntosh's successor) and Keith Holyoake (Prime Minister and Minister of External Affairs) that he had been a diplomat for only eleven years, that he was just getting into his stride in Germany, and that the German authorities had indicated strongly that they hoped he would remain in Bonn.

All to no avail. He was recalled and, in 1969, retired. His disappointment was exacerbated by the fact that when he applied for the newly created full-time directorship of the Institute of International Affairs, he was passed over in favour of Bruce Brown, a diplomat twenty-seven years his junior. This juxtaposition of events sowed seeds that would germinate poisonously in his mind.

And so, somewhat reluctantly, Reuel and Dorothy headed for Auckland, where their son Mark lived with his family, and bought and extended their dream house at Whangaparaoa. There they commenced a life of study, writing, music and entertaining. And there, over the next decade, Reuel waged a series of campaigns that would come to be seen as the cause — or perhaps the symptoms — of his mental deterioration.

The first crisis, a further encounter with the Institute of International Affairs, was unfolding at about the time I met him. Reuel had had a long association with that body. He had joined it and first addressed its members in 1935. The institute had had sufficient confidence in his judgement in 1951 to co-publish his book on immigration. He was a close friend of the president, Sir Guy Powles. The length and strength of these associations had made the rejection of his application for the directorship in 1968 all the more disappointing.

In 1970, two Cambodian delegations — one parliamentary, one student — visited New Zealand and Lochore tried to arrange institute-sponsored meetings for both in Auckland and Wellington. When these efforts came to nothing, he decided that the institute's lack of interest was an "act of censorship" on the part of what was by now the

Department of Foreign Affairs. Senior members of Foreign Affairs, he believed, did not support the political factions represented by the delegations and were communicating their disapproval through institute policy via Bruce Brown who was on secondment from the department.

Shortly afterwards, in 1971, Lochore submitted to the institute for publication a manuscript on Vietnamese expansion in South-East Asia. It was rejected. The same year the Cambodian Foreign Minister Koun Wick visited New Zealand and Lochore was prevented by official escorts from speaking to him at a public function in Auckland. These events convinced him that he had been blacklisted by the institute and by his old department.

But Lochore took matters further. He examined the publications of the institute since the time of Bruce Brown's appointment and judged that their common denominator was their acceptability to the Department of Foreign Affairs and their compatibility with the policies of the Peking-aligned New Zealand Communist Party. From this he deduced that the department was under communist control (and he eventually traced this back to the recruitment policies of Sir Alister McIntosh); as was the Institute of International Affairs through the department's control of its directors. After a series of clashes with the institute's Auckland committee arising from his insistence on this scenario, Lochore eventually withdrew his membership.

His second major arena for public dispute was his research into what he referred to as "the Mesopotamian origins of the Polynesians". This thesis, based on prodigious analysis of language, archaeological findings and mythology, was first floated in his Hocken Lecture at Otago University in 1973 (published in 1974): *Culture-Historical Aspects Of The Malayo-Polynesian Settlement In Ancient South-East Asia.*

He argued that the Polynesians had evolved in Northern Mesopotamia, which he identified as the "Uru" homeland of Takitimu Maori tradition. He claimed that these people had migrated out of the Middle East by two routes, one seaward and one land, and made their way to South-East Asia and thence to the Pacific.

Two years later, after correspondence with Barry Fell, a New Zealander who was Professor of Invertebrate Zoology at Harvard University and who claimed to be able to decipher ancient Middle Eastern inscriptions, Lochore modified his hypothesis to suggest that the earlier landward migration had proceeded directly from Mesopotamia to the

Pacific; while the seaward one had gone via Libya.

These theories were in conflict with the work of every recognised specialist in Pacific history and prehistory. Anthropologists, archaeologists and linguists believe that the Polynesians evolved in the central South Pacific, from people who had migrated there earlier from South-East Asia. Lochore's attempt to link Maori mythology with that of the Middle East and to seek coincidental language affinities over a period of 5000 years was not only seen as unsound, it was regarded as academic quackery.

Not one reputable scholar in New Zealand, Australia, the United States or Europe came forward to support Lochore and Fell's views. Cranks emerged in large numbers, however, and Lochore, grateful for their support — for any support — tended to clutch at every item of loopy evidence that amateur sleuths sent him (such as "proof" that the taiaha had come from Egypt, originally as a metal weapon).

He elaborated his original scenario to the point where he compiled a detailed "history" of the Polynesians — in the Middle East, South-East Asia, the Pacific and North America — from 3100 BC to 400 AD. It was from this morass of information, fertilised further by Barry Fell, that an astonishing account emerged of "Maui, a Libyan navigator who, in the second century BC, set out to circumnavigate the world but finished up exploring the Pacific and the western coasts of North and South America".

It was fascinating stuff and the public at large loved it. Most New Zealand newspapers and magazines such as the *Listener* carried variations on the story between 1975 and 1977, attributing it to Fell or Lochore or both. A New Zealand film maker announced a forthcoming motion picture on Maui the Libyan and Polynesian culture hero.

It was also nonsense. Academics and museum spokespersons attacked Lochore in print and at public meetings in Auckland, and he became convinced that there was now a university conspiracy to blacklist him, as virulent as that emanating from the Department of Foreign Affairs.

He wrote to me in 1977, summarising the path his research had taken and asking me to support his conclusions and continue the project. "In two years you could have the best qualifications in the world to take a chair of Polynesian linguistics in a New Zealand university." I had to decline this offer of preferment. Whenever we were together and he began to embark on this topic, I had to work hard to change the subject.

He was immune to evidence to the contrary or even to commonsense. Dorothy, who had previously been a loyal supporter, began to look worried when these conversations occurred.

By 1978 Reuel was embarked on a new preoccupation. He became convinced that Prime Minister Robert Muldoon was planning to provoke civil unrest so as to use the Public Safety and Conservation Act to assume dictatorial powers. Already, he alleged, executive power was concentrated in the hands of Muldoon, Frank Gill and National Party president George Chapman. Muldoon had supposedly declared that the Labour opposition would never again be allowed to form a government and he appeared to be using the SIS to obtain information on political opponents. In November, Reuel believed that the army and air force had been put on night exercises around Auckland to discourage a disgruntled populace from rising up and revolting in the course of that month's general election.

He fired off correspondence about aspects of this conspiracy to Sir John Marshall (who he believed would intervene and form an alternative government) and to a variety of newspapers. Most did not publish his letters, which only served to convince him that Muldoon's control now extended to the news media.

About this time, too, Lochore made the acquaintance of other Aucklanders who could be said to occupy the extreme right of the New Zealand political spectrum: Clark Titman, the strident anti-communist, and Ned Haliburton of Orewa, who claimed to be a Scottish peer and a former employee of the British intelligence services. With Haliburton, Barry Reed, Barbara Faithfull and other ultra-conservatives, Reuel Lochore became a founder member of Credo, a so-called media watchdog group.

The first Lochore-Haliburton initiative was a 1980 submission to Parliament's unsuspecting Statutes Revision Committee. This alleged that British KGB agents had infiltrated the public service to supply drugs to New Zealand and bring about the collapse of law, order and government. The submission claimed that the Soviet-inspired campaign was centred on the departments of Foreign Affairs, Trade and Industry, Defence, Justice and Health. It said Dr Lochore knew the identities of fifteen of the agents and that their names had been passed to the Security Intelligence Service.

Two years later, Lochore's now fully fledged communist conspiracy theory was presented to another select committee, the Commerce and

Energy Committee, as part of a Credo submission on the Broadcasting Amendment Bill.

This extraordinary document claimed that the "founder-leader" of the KGB in New Zealand was Lochore's old boss, Sir Alister McIntosh, who had died in 1978. From 1946, according to Lochore, McIntosh had brought a series of KGB agents into the Prime Minister's Department and External Affairs, beginning with Paddy Costello, who had been first secretary in the New Zealand Legation in Moscow. McIntosh's only rival for the leadership of the local moles had been Dr W B Sutch, who had not succeeded because he was not as "sagacious" as McIntosh.

After McIntosh had built up his network, Lochore continued, he turned his attention to the infiltration of the New Zealand broadcasting services. This sideways move was made possible by the Kirk Government's Committee on Broadcasting, which — Lochore alleged — was made up of "academic Marxists". It was they who engineered the appointment in 1973 of McIntosh as chairman of the Broadcasting Council, and McIntosh in turn placed further KGB agents throughout the radio and television networks. McIntosh's instructions to these moles, Lochore said, were: "First target broadcasting, second the rest of the media, third the nation."

McIntosh's death did not end the campaign. Lochore alleged that it was taken over by Ian Cross who, Lochore believed, was less successful than McIntosh because he was less astute.

Unsurprisingly, nobody took any official action in response to these warnings. They proved too bizarre even for *Truth*, which declined to publish them, and over the next two years Reuel Lochore became increasingly distressed and obsessed, believing that the communist tentacles were spreading unchecked. He wrote letters to ministers of the Crown and newspapers almost weekly. These too were largely ignored. When, as gently as I could, I too turned down his appeal for support, he became convinced that I was part of the conspiracy and not to be trusted.

By 1984 his delusions had driven Lochore to a surprising conclusion. The only people who could save New Zealand, he believed, were the Maori, particularly the Maori nationalists. "The one adequate remedy," he wrote to a Member of Parliament, "is to return to the Maori sufficient tribal lands for him to develop his own tribal economy (including exports) and bilingual system of education . . . Subject should be publicised with caution, Pakeha resistance being considerable."

Ignored by officialdom, or — worse — made the subject of polite and impolite put-offs, Lochore decided to make one last dramatic gesture. He would bring his country's plight to world attention. He would visit Australia and brief the new Labour Prime Minister Bob Hawke, and trust that the anti-communist Hawke would take international action to rid New Zealand of the cancer that was subverting its people and institutions.

And so, in September 1984, Reuel Lochore flew to Sydney. Asked the purpose of his visit by an immigration official, he told him, in considerable detail. The official invited him to step into an interview room, where the New Zealander was given a cup of coffee and asked to wait. Eventually a psychiatrist arrived to assess him. After a long discussion, the psychiatrist assured Lochore that his warnings would be passed on to the Prime Minister and that Australia need detain him no longer. His return trip was pre-booked for three days later, however. Immigration officials checked him into a Sydney hotel, kept him under surveillance for three days, then escorted him to the airport for his flight home.

In 1985 I rang to say I was coming to visit. Dorothy, distressed and unwell, said that Reuel had "gone to Otaki to see the Maori Queen". The following day I rang back. "But the Maori Queen doesn't live at Otaki," I told her. "Yes," said Dorothy. "Reuel rang last night and said he couldn't find her." I wondered at this time if he ought to be in care, or at least under some kind of medical supervision. But I felt that it wasn't my place to suggest this. And he was at least taking care of Dorothy, whose health was deteriorating.

It was Dorothy who had to go into care that same year, however. The following year, 1986, Reuel had a stroke which left him further disabled, mentally and physically, and he moved to North Haven Hospital.

By now he had a new obsession: Margaret Thatcher, who had spoken in the House of Commons in defence of Roger Hollis, was clearly behind all the conspiracies. He believed that she too had sent agents to New Zealand to murder the elderly and the wise, and to take over the country. At night he heard the streets ringing with the sounds of booted feet. The Maori, he believed still, were New Zealand's only hope.

"Dear Madame and Jewel of Ngati Porou," he wrote to Atareta Poananga, in one of his last, crazy letters. "I am an ex-Pakeha trying to become a good Maori. Now my work is interrupted by the incursions of the devil-woman Thatcher into East Asia. She pressed English schoolboys of fifteen years to settle in Aotearoa and learn the use of the short-barrelled carbine for genocide. We estimate their total number at 200,000 . . . There are a multitude of possible answers to that challenge, and I suggest we should take up those which are most acceptable and rewarding to our Maori People of Aotearoa."

He addressed the letter to the only Poananga he could find in the Auckland telephone directory: Atareta's mother, who happens to be Pakeha.

Later that year, 1987, Dorothy died. Reuel continued his slide into fear and confusion until — at last — he could no longer remember the things that had troubled him for so long. From that point, looking content again, he lived — and lives — in a continuous and featureless present.

⌒

Reuel Lochore's obsessive and wrong-headed views about communism and the Mesopotamian origins of the Maori are matters of record. No one disputes that he held them. At best, they can be seen as symptoms of a mind collapsing under the burdens of age and anxiety; at worst, they are an illustration of the truth of Moliere's maxim quoted in reference to Reuel by his tolerant cousin, Geoff Alley: "There's no fool like a clever fool."

More sinister, however, and outside the period for which mental deteriorations can be cited as a mitigating factor, is the suggestion that the man was a fascist. This accusation was first made by newspaper correspondents in the 1930s after Lochore had begun his series of public lectures about his experiences in Germany. It was repeated when he supported von Luckner's visit in 1938, and again when he was thought by some to have been too rigorous in his interviewing of European refugees.

Apart from letters-to-the-editor in 1935, these allegations were made largely in private conversation (and, in one instance, in an obscene letter sent to Lochore in 1938). I heard them in the 1970s, when people in Wellington discovered that I knew him. They became public knowledge in 1990 with the publication of the autobiography of Czech-refugee industrialist Fred Turnovsky.

In *Fifty Years In New Zealand*, Turnovsky recounts how he and his wife Lotte had difficulties obtaining naturalisation in 1946, six years after they had landed in the country. He describes an interview with officers of the Department of Internal Affairs:

". . . the man across the table seemed an innocuous bureaucrat asking innocuous questions; behind him sat a shadowy figure who at first said nothing, but soon took over the questioning. What I thought would be a formal interview turned into an interrogation, in the course of which he questioned everything even remotely connected with me, not least my integrity and political credibility. Was I or had I ever been a comm-unist? Could I prove my Social-Democrat connection? (I did.) Being a Czechoslovak citizen, was I able to speak Czech? (I said Czech was my mother tongue.) Why did I not associate more with the Jewish community? (I had no answer to that; I felt no obligation to explain to him that my preferences lay in different directions.) This inquisition took on Kafkaesque proportions, and continued for what seemed an eternity . . ."

The Turnovskys eventually acquired New Zealand citizenship. But Fred Turnovsky tried to find out more about the man who had put him through an unpleasant experience: Dr R A Lochore. He read the book *From Europe To New Zealand* and found "some outrageous statements with strong ethnic, or to use the more commonplace term, racist overtones . . ." He detected a similarity between Lochore's attitude towards British and Nordic peoples and Hitler's view of "das Herrenvolk — the master race . . . Was Lochore transposing an admiration for Hitler's Germany into a New Zealand setting?"

Further research uncovered the fact that Lochore had spent a week "in 1936 [sic]" lecturing to a camp of Nazi storm-troopers; and that he had been a sponsor of von Luckner's visit "in 1937 [sic]". Von Luckner, Lochore had said, would show that "Germans are not the barbarians and sadists that fanatical war propaganda and its aftermath have so luridly depicted". (He was speaking, of course, of World War One propaganda.) Turnovsky comments: "It would appear that it was [Lochore] who became indoctrinated with Nazi ideals during his stay in the storm-trooper camp . . ."

Worse was to come. Turnovsky found clearly anti-Semitic references in the original manuscript of *From Europe To New Zealand*. These had been edited out of the published version. One alleged that "the worst thing about the Jewish people is . . . that they cringe and fawn when they are weak, and bully and exploit when they have power . . . There is the Jew's uncanny ability to see always one move ahead of his competitors . . ." Turnovsky comments that such allusions read as if they were inspired by *Der Sturmer*, the satirical journal which had set out in the 1930s to depict Jews in the worst possible light.

Finally, Turnovsky refers to Lochore's appointment as Ambassador to West Germany as "the ultimate irony . . . A few years ago West Germany appointed an ambassador to Wellington, but withdrew him immediately when it was revealed that he had been a member of the SS during the war. Lochore's appointment did not receive such attention. I asked some foreign affairs veterans how McIntosh, reported to be a man of vision with a liberal disposition, could have been a party to such an appointment, but nobody was able to give me a satisfactory explanation."

The explanation is, of course, that McIntosh, who knew Lochore well for more than thirty years, did not believe that he was or ever had been a Nazi sympathiser. I know this because I asked McIntosh about Lochore in the course of a series of interviews in 1978. McIntosh's view then was that Lochore was "a bit potty, but a brilliant linguist. He was also a good analyst and an exceptionally good draftsman."

While the scenario Turnovsky constructs is plausible, (though some of his dates are wrong), it does not stand up to scrutiny.

It is true that Lochore spent time with the storm-troopers and with the Hitler Youth Movement in Germany, and that he was presented with their insignia; it is true that he mingled and talked with Nazis. His own explanation of this, however, made frequently in the course of his New Zealand lectures in 1935, is that it was part of his brief to "study the contemporary social and cultural condition of the German people".

"I am no Fascist, no admirer of Hitler," he wrote to the *Evening Post* in a letter published on 1 July 1935. "Did I state or insinuate that there is no terror in Germany? I lived in Germany from August 1930 to January 1935, with Jews in Berlin, with Nazis in Mainz, with Freemasons in Bonn, with Nationalists in the Ruhr. I have myself been manhandled by Nazis and received attention from the German political police. I do not need to learn from your correspondents what terrorism in Germany is."

Lochore described the "manhandling" in some detail in an interview broadcast on the YC network in 1981:

"In my first fortnight in Berlin . . . I found myself in a crowd of people who were very excited . . . As this boy came near me and offered me a leaflet, everybody around about said, 'No, no, don't take it.' I didn't take any notice. I took one. A man turned on me and said, 'Sind Sie kommunist?' I said, 'Kommunist nein. Ich bin Auslander.' I'm a foreigner, that's all. And then they started pummelling me from all sides. I threw my weight about and made a little bit of a clearance round me and stood up to them and said plainly, 'Ich bin Auslander. Ich bin nicht Deutsch. Ich verstehe nicht was Sie tun.' I'm a foreigner, not a German. I don't understand what you're doing. I was all ready to have an argument with them about this . . . But a man just behind me said, 'Look, get out.' He opened a way through the crowd for me to get away . . . I did it. I wasn't seriously hurt. But I got my first inkling of what was going to happen in Germany from that."

Lochore's extreme distaste for Nazism is also clear in his correspondence with his family. In a letter to his mother in January 1935 he refers to Hitler as "a fanatic demagogue" and to the Fuhrer's "shallow racial mysticism. I must say it is a relief to be out of Germany. Although this nationalist development was inevitable and largely our own fault, I cannot but forebode evil from the doctrines that are being inculcated there, and hope they will soon be toned down. If you preach to a nation long enough that all the others are rogues . . . something untoward is bound to happen."

Lochore's difficulty, and the factor that caused people to mistrust him, was that although he condemned Nazism, he nonetheless believed that its growth was a consequence of conditions imposed by the Allies on Germany in the wake of World War One. He also believed in the mid-1930s that the country was most likely to be led back to civilised behaviour if the international community retained its trade and cultural links with Germany. His so-called "secret mission" in 1935, which he took to the New Zealand Government, was a proposal that New Zealand enter a barter agreement to exchange butter and wool for German manufactured goods.

"Germany today is mad; we helped to drive her mad," he wrote in 1935. "If we have any Christianity in us, we have to try to restore her sanity. The way to do that is to offer her our friendship. That is also the way to end terrorism in Germany; for advice is often accepted from a candid friend, but never from a moralist who preaches from a Pharisaic pedestal . . . I have written out of affection for a great and noble nation, and out of the will to bring order into world affairs."

This argument is strikingly similar to the one that proposed "building bridges" with South Africa in the 1960s and 1970s. It is equally naive, and it was rightly condemned in some quarters in the mid-1930s. But it is not tantamount to support of Nazism.

In fact, once New Zealand *was* fighting Germany, nobody supported the war more vigorously than Reuel Lochore. His notes on interviewing, prepared for the Aliens Tribunals, which produced the kind of grilling of which Turnovsky complained, make it clear that he was ruthless in his determination to ensure that people with Nazi sympathies were not considered eligible for New Zealand citizenship. In January 1940 he resigned his subscription to the journal *Tomorrow* in protest at the fact that some of its contributors were opposed to the war, because of the Russian-German non-aggression pact.

"Sir," he wrote then, "we are at war; and there is only one thing to do about a war — to win it. All nuances of opinion must be temporarily resolved into the plain black-and-white of pro or contra. Let your brittle intellectuals give up their New Year resolutions and build up a national will to victory; or let them try to sabotage this country's war effort, if they dare . . ."

His sponsorship of von Luckner's visit was an example not of support of fascism but of naivety. He believed that the count was not a Nazi (and indeed von Luckner's behaviour and treatment during World War Two established that he was not). And — whatever propaganda advantages the German Government was able to derive from the swashbuckling aristocrat's lecture tours — Lochore believed simply that he represented the best of Germany's values and ideals. He wrote to his mother from Munich in January 1935:

". . . by a piece of supreme good luck, I struck Count von Luckner (you remember him during the war?) . . . he lectured last night to the Stablehelm in Nuremberg. Of course I went, and was so struck by him (as everyone is) that I pushed up to him, told him I was from New Zealand, and asked him when he was coming back to see us. He was very keen, and his wife too, and they will come if finance can be arranged: something else for me to potter about with . . . when I get back. He would take New Zealand by storm as he did USA where he has been combating war propaganda for seven years past . . . His motto is 'chivalry and humanity'. . . ."

Accusations about Lochore's anti-Semitism seem persuasive, especially in the light of pro-Nazi sympathies. Once the Nazi allegations are disposed of, however, and the record of Lochore's wider beliefs and activities are considered, his comments about Jews in the manuscript of *From Europe To New Zealand* seem more silly than sinister. His writings are full of equally sweeping and foolish generalisations about other peoples and cultures. He wrote of the Chinese, for example:

"[They] are an overrated nation. They pretend to a history of 6000 years, but it is actually less than 4000. They are full of conceit and have little to be conceited about. . . . Their science is mere rule-of-thumb. They failed to invent even a syllabic alphabet. . . . Their art consists of [mere] decorative stuff. Their music is hideous. . . . Their medicine is quackery. . . ."

Or, of the Italians:

"You can certainly get along by bullying them, but you can get along just as well by talking in a loud but friendly voice. Whereas if you don't assert yourself at all they simply overlook your existence."

This is John Cleese territory.

More importantly, in his articles, talks and letters, Lochore was as critical of Germany's anti-Jewish practices as anybody. He wrote from Munich:

"The notorious Julius Streicher, inventor of those fables about Jewish ritual sacrifices, is the big man in Bavaria, and here I have several times seen the sign on pub doors: 'No admittance for Jews' . . . I'll never go into a shop that has that sign up."

During the war, disturbed by evidence of New Zealand prejudice against Jewish refugees, Lochore wrote an article for the *Listener,* asking for tolerance of this group and emphasising the contribution they were making to New Zealand life and culture. He referred to the Nazi view of Jewishness as "a freak definition based on racial mysticism". He went on to say:

"All refugees hate Hitler. Refugees are here because there was no place for them in Hitler's Europe. Over half of them have near relatives who were unable to escape in time, and are therefore now in the ghetto camps of Poland. There are no mail connections with these camps, no news ever comes out via the Red Cross, but as for the aged and infirm, the refugee's only hope is that his dear ones died quickly and easily. . . . [They] have had only two possible choices: either to make a new home overseas, or to get into war against the dictators, and to purge [their] country . . . with fire and slaughter. . . . Yet many New Zealanders seem to think that refugees are secretly pro-Nazi."

This article, published in May 1944 before the full truth was known about the Nazi extermination camps, reveals a concern for the plight of Jewish refugees far in advance of that held by New Zealanders in general. It produced a flood of approving letters to Lochore from such refugees, once it became known that he had written it.

Further, for someone alleged to be anti-Semitic, he had an extraordinary number of Jewish friends: the Plischkes, the Fleischls, Paul Heller, Maria Dronke. Indeed, Hilda and Mario Fleischl are specifically thanked for "assistance and encouragement" in the acknowledgments for *From Europe To New Zealand*. Dorothy Lochore had even deeper roots into the Jewish community: from her continuing friendship with the Schnabel family (who had been forced to flee Italy to escape fascist persecution), to the other two musicians in her Dorothy Davies Trio. Their daughter-in-law too was Jewish, and no less loved for that reason.

In the course of researching this memoir I spoke to a wide range of people who had known Reuel Lochore over many decades. All were embarrassed and distressed by the wild campaigns that marked his later years. None believed that he had been a Nazi or Nazi sympathiser, however, nor that his so-called anti-Semitism amounted to anything more than a characteristic brand of ethnocentrism. Those who had lived in his household, especially his Davies nephews, recall him expressly condemning fascism and anti-Semitism.

Some, such as Sir Charles Bennett, were almost incoherent with indignation about the allegations in the Turnovsky book. "Reuel was an odd chap," says Bennett who was high commissioner in Malaya when Lochore was first secretary, and who kept in close touch with him in later years. "He had some peculiar opinions and mannerisms. But he was a solid and reliable man who gave absolute loyalty to his country, to his job, to his superiors. I have, and had then, nothing but the highest praise for his character. He gave me a great deal of strength in my position because his advice was astute and disinterested, and because I knew I could depend on him one hundred percent."

I have tried to write honestly about Reuel Lochore's strengths and weaknesses, and to draw conclusions from the evidence rather than from my personal affection for him and Dorothy Davies. I believe the view reflected in the Turnovsky book is not without justification, because of the enormous number of forthright and frequently foolish opinions expressed by Lochore in the course of a long professional life. But the same record that, on partial acquaintance, condemns him, also comes to his rescue.

A reading of everything that Lochore wrote — in letters published and unpublished, diaries, articles, talks, public service reports — leaves one in no doubt that he was, at worst, a voluble and volatile eccentric of conservative inclination. At best, however, he was a man who tried to apply reason and ethics to the affairs of his time, and to ensure that those affairs were debated widely. His tragedy is that he lived long enough for his wits to disintegrate and thus obliterate much of the good that he did in his public and private lives.

&

The Duke of Dysfunction

This memoir of the New Zealand-born sexologist John Money was written for the Listener, *4 April 1998, after American media had accused Money of promoting mutilation, brainwashing and kiddy porn.*

THE IMPOVERISHED NEIGHBOURHOODS of north-east Baltimore are among the least prepossessing in the United States. The "row houses" — "terraced" in English idiom — are made of decaying brick. Iron gratings frame the windows. Doors customarily have an assortment of locks and bolts. Everywhere the ground is covered in asphalt, cracked concrete and litter. Almost the only greenery is the odd weed that sprouts in concrete crevices.

The corner store is built like a bank. Provisions are piled behind a grille. You give your order to the grocer through bulletproof glass. You put your money through a levered slot, which he reverses to convey your purchases. According to one observer, the district has "one murder every day and many more robberies and muggings with violence, both random and familial . . ."

Strange, then, that it should be the chosen home of one of the few white professional men on the block. Dr John Money lives in another corner shop, now converted into a residence. Strange, too, that he has grown a garden inside the projecting front window, so that the effect from the outside is like looking into a tropical aquarium. Behind the plants, the bottom floor is crammed with Australian Aboriginal and

African wood sculptures and masks that give the interior the appearance of a voodoo parlour.

Morrinsville-born Money was one of the people Margaret Mead had in mind when she declared that New Zealand's role was to "send out its bright young men and women to run the rest of the world". He's no longer young: he will be seventy-seven this year. But he was when he abandoned Dunedin for the US in 1947 to do postgraduate work in psychology at Pittsburgh and Harvard. And he was and is bright, dazzlingly so. As director of the Psychohormonal Research Unit at Johns Hopkins University, he is widely recognised as the world's leading sexologist, successor to the mantles of Freud, Kinsey and Masters and Johnson. Film-maker John Waters dubs him the "Duke of Dysfunction" for his ground-breaking work with sex offenders.

So what's he doing living in one of the most blighted urban neighbourhoods in North America? It suits him, he says. The property was cheap when he bought it thirty-five years ago. It was within walking distance of Johns Hopkins (although, having been mugged, he no longer walks). Why should he shift just because others of his race and class have abandoned the district? It seems a very "New Zealand" attitude, assertive, verging on defiant.

His immediate neighbours are protective and respectful, and their children call him "Mr Doc". And Money knows how to handle life on the street. One evening, as he winds down his car window in preparation for edging onto the road, a local youth with excited eyes inserts his torso and reaches for my bag on the back seat. Money, who knows him, thrusts a hand under the intruder's chin and shoves hard. "F— off, motherf—er," he says emphatically. The youth stands there rubbing his chin and watching us move out from the curb. Then he waves and calls out, with no sign of hostility, "You take care, motherf—ers." Just another example of Baltimore slum discourse. The vocabulary may be limited, but it accelerates understanding.

⌒

I'm visiting John Money because of his fifty-year association with the New Zealand writer Janet Frame. He is the dashing young psychology lecturer featured in volume two of Frame's autobiography, *An Angel At My Table*, as John Forrest. "He was handsome, fairhaired with a lock of hair draped over his forehead [and] wore a rust-coloured sports coat and tomato-red socks . . . 'How do you like my tomayto socks?'"

A character in some respects based on Money turns up again in Frame's novel, *Living In The Maniototo*. This time, he is Dr Brian Wilford, who runs a clinic for dyslexics in Baltimore:

"Brian was an accurate man, and already my many inaccuracies were beginning to irritate him. This evening, however, he had more on his mind. On his recent travels to a conference he had bought himself an elaborate watch, the temporal equivalent of a hotdog 'with everything on it', but unfortunately it was five years ahead in time . . . The only thing to do, we supposed, was to wind the watch back through the hours and days and years. Patiently.

"We had a late supper. At half-past one in the morning, Brian was still rewinding his watch, every now and again giving details of his progress or regress. 'Only three years to go.' 'Two years.' 'My fingers are worn out. There must be some other way.' (He found out later that there was.)

". . . Finally in the early hours of the morning, Brian had shed those five years of inadvertent time and was back in the present."

Between the years of those literary portraits, Money's career progress was meteoric. In 1951, he moved from Harvard to Johns Hopkins, where he founded the Psychohormonal Research Unit and, just over a decade later, the Gender Identity Clinic. He was the pioneer in the treatment of hermaphroditic or "intersex" children by programmes of sexual assignment, which often involved surgery, hormonal treatment and counselling. He was involved in sexual-reassignment programmes for transsexuals. He coined and defined the now widely used terms "gender role" and "lovemap". He made major contributions to theoretical understandings of homosexuality, bisexuality and heterosexuality. And he devised successful psychological and hormonal programmes for the treatment of so-called sexual deviants, for whose often kinky disorders he revived the word "paraphilia". He taught generations of medical students at Johns Hopkins. And he has written or co-authored about forty books and nearly four hundred scientific papers. The value of his work has been recognised not only in the professional literature, but also in such publications as *Time* and the *New York Times*. He has turned up on *The Oprah Winfrey Show* and in *Playboy*.

Money's commitment to research and proselytising shows no sign of diminution in his eighth decade. Although he is now a professor emeritus of medical psychology and paediatrics, he still runs the psychohormonal unit at Johns Hopkins and puts in twelve hours a day at the university. Indeed, his office, with its books, pleasant furniture, pot plants and artwork, seems more "homely" than his home — although the university, a teaching hospital, is built like a fortress and staff are often escorted between carpark and office by security guards.

Money still travels the world to present provocative papers at sex conferences (when I arrived in Baltimore, he had just returned from Valencia). He still runs a weekly clinic for therapists and researchers from Maryland, Virginia and Washington, DC — and for those from further afield who can get there. One woman attending this clinic the week I was there clasps my hand and says, with the kind of sincerity that only Americans can get away with, "You've no idea what a privilege it is to work with a man like John."

Indeed, Money is one of those rare scholars and teachers who are blessed with charisma. He is well organised in his gathering and presentation of data, tenacious in argument; but also playful in the way in which he draws people out. Health professionals and patients appear either to admire him intensely or dislike him just as strongly. With Dr Money, it seems, there is no middle ground.

I'm one of the admirers. I much enjoy his energy, his generosity and his hospitality (which includes impromptu evening performances on his home piano). His openness to experience and his willingness to take on the rest of the world in argument on a myriad issues, without being intimidated by the reputations of his adversaries, seem to me to be very New Zealand qualities. John Money could have been one of those John Mulgan had in mind when he wrote, "Everything that was good from that small, remote country had gone into them — sunshine and strength, good sense, patience, the versatility of practical men."

But such judgments are not universal. Within weeks of my staying with him, a storm broke that perfectly illustrates the divisive potential of the Money methods and style. It began with the March 1997 issue of the American Medical Association's *Archives of Paediatrics and Adolescent Medicine*. There a long-time professional opponent, University of Hawaii biologist Mickey Diamond, and Keith Sigmundson, a young Canadian psychiatrist, challenged the methodology and conclusions of one of Money's most famous cases: that of a Canadian twin boy whose penis had been burnt off in a circumcision accident, who was reassigned a female gender in his home city and who was sent to Johns Hopkins for surgery and further treatment.

According to Diamond and Sigmundson, what they called the "John/Joan" case was an experiment, it had not worked and it severely traumatised the patient. Worse, they implied that Money had mis-reported his follow-up counselling and investigation sessions. What the "experiment" revealed, they alleged, was the opposite conclusion to that promulgated by Money: gender identity and sexual orientation are not malleable; they are inborn; and, while rearing may play a role in shaping sexual identity, biology is a far stronger force than "nurture".

The accusations were repeated in the *New York Times* on 14 March 1997, and in an excoriating article by journalist John Colapinto in the 11 December 1997 issue of the magazine *Rolling Stone*. Colapinto added new accusations, that Money championed "open marriage, nudism and the dissemination of explicit pornography". Simultaneously, the 8 December issue of the Rupert Murdoch-owned *New York Post* editorialised that fifteen thousand American children had been mutilated in the previous twenty-five years, "not by perverts, but by trained surgeons". The *Post* went on:

"They decide on a sex for the child, remove the genitalia that do not agree with their decision and complete the picture with surgical construction. Boy, girl; it's all the same, as long as society's brainwashing does its job. The ascendancy of this bizarre practice is due to one man, the world-renowned Johns Hopkins Psychiatrist [sic] John Money. . . .

"Money had always been as much of a polemicist as a psychiatrist. A self-described 'missionary' of sex, he has also advocated bisexual orgies and pederasty. Now that Money's work is discredited, sexual radicals will likely latch onto some new piece of junk science to support their notions. But it's not just the science that was junk. It is the theory itself. And in pursuit of that theory, John Money mutilated babies."

Personal and professional criticism doesn't come any stronger than that. But is it justified? Even to a layman, there are holes apparent in the fabric of the critique. One is the fact that one case out of thousands is being used to challenge Money's whole career. And it is an untypical case — virtually all the sex-assignment operations and treatments with which Money was associated were carried out on children with birth defects of the sex organs, or adults who wished to change their sex. And they were carried out by a team at Johns Hopkins, not Money alone. Second, Colapinto criticises Money both for trying to carry out follow-up reporting of the "John/Joan" case in the face of patient opposition and then for not doing so as a result of that opposition.

A third and major weakness of the Colapinto and *New York Post* argument is the use of emotional and pejorative terms to describe treatment: surgery becomes "mutilation"; therapy "brainwashing"; pictures of genitals shown to children to demonstrate normal anatomy become "kiddy porn". And nowhere do the *Rolling Stone* or *New York Post* pieces make it clear that "John/Joan" was reassigned a female gender before she came to Johns Hopkins and was operated on at what Money regarded as an undesirably late age (twenty-two months).

Nor do the critical articles make it clear why sexual-assignment treatment was carried out. It was not to gratify perverted doctors with vampirish appetites. It was to relieve the sufferings of individuals and families unable to answer that basic question: is it a boy or a girl? It was to remove hermaphroditic people from the freak category, which had formerly relegated some of them to circuses and side-shows and led to lives of misery, social isolation and even persecution.

When I telephone Money to see how *he* is coping with the accusations, which others might see as an attempt to destroy a reputation and a career, I find him surprisingly resilient and sanguine. Mickey Diamond has been gunning for him for thirty years. It's not a new obsession. And there's more going on than meets the eye. *New York* magazine has reported that Colapinto has received a $450,000 advance from HarperCollins, and that Hollywood is showing an interest in the story.

Money notes also that the *Rolling Stone* piece is shot through with errors of quotation and manufactured evidence. He's not going to recite the list, nor reply in detail. To do so, he says, would take a vast amount of time to retrack and document. It's not what he planned to do with this time of his life. And litigation, even if successful, would be hugely expensive, especially given the resources of a Murdoch-owned publication. It would also be emotionally corrosive. Further, to re-open the records and quote from them would require patient and family consent. And he's unlikely to get that from the patient and family who are the focus for the current quarrel.

As for the administrators of Johns Hopkins, they appear to view the Diamond/Colapinto revelations as simply one more controversy in a career characterised by controversy. They have heard all this before. They believe that the most effective response is to ignore the attack and not to fan the flames by taking these people on in public or in court. But Money is still taking advice on the legal issues. It's a fair assumption that publishers and film-makers who want to take the story further may receive lawyers' letters.

It's apparent to anyone who knows him that, in some respects, John Money can seem to be his own worst enemy. To compensate for the puritan and repressive mores of his upbringing (family membership of a Brethren church in small New Zealand towns such as Morrinsville), he often uses colloquial expressions for sexual activity: "f—ing" and "jacking-off", for example, where other clinical practitioners would more often say "intercourse" or "masturbation". Some of his book titles are playfully provocative: *Venuses Penuses: Sexology, Sexosophy and Exigency Theory*; or *The Breathless Orgasm: A Lovemap Biography of Asphyxiophilia*. And he has allowed publication of pictures of himself — in magazines and on the cover of his 1994 volume *Re-interpreting the Unspeakable* — in which the photography has succeeded in making him look sinister.

All these things have provoked negative responses from those of the Moral Majority ilk and convinced them that, in Money, they are confronted by a monster of depravity. Such behaviour has also made Money and his work vastly appealing to journalists and allowed him to carry on his discourse on sexual matters far beyond the professional literature and out into the mainstream media. They are the source of his appeal to the likes of Oprah Winfrey and *Playboy*.

Money's professional reputation and celebrity profile were at their highest point during the sexual revolution of the 1960s and 1970s. Then, he was widely honoured as a prophet whose time had come. In the climate of the 1990s, when a new puritanism has been fuelled by the Aids epidemic and the rise of the so-called Moral Majority in small-town America, he is sometimes cast as a promoter of sexual promiscuity rather than what any fair assessment of his career reveals him to be: an extraordinarily gifted healer of sexual dysfunction.

The worst that Money has been "guilty" of is advocating and pursuing the right of everybody who wants it to a happy and fulfilling gender identity and sex life. His work on the effect of social conditioning on gender has been a major force underpinning contemporary feminist theory. The vast corpus of his theories and therapies relating to a wide range of sexual behaviour, he notes, is not under challenge by health professionals. Indeed, he has recently been recommended for a grant from the American National Institutes of Health for a major new project, a classification and consolidation of contemporary knowledge of paraphilias or "perversions".

And, from the thousands of successful cases of sexual assignment and reassignment with which he has been associated, has grown a network of appreciative families, many of whom remain in contact with Money. Janet Frame recalls accompanying him to a large Jewish wedding just outside Baltimore in which the groom was the product of "successful" reassignment therapy in infancy. Without that therapy, there would have been no wedding, no grounds for an extended family celebration.

It may be a long time before the verdict is in on that old chestnut, the nature versus nurture debate. Few scientists now plump for one factor to the exclusion of the other: disagreement is now based on emphasis and proportion. Money's view, borne out by his own work, is that nature needs nurture, that neither can exist without the other. That is why he continues to fight the Mickey Diamond hypothesis that the influence of nature is paramount, that "biology is destiny". The big issue, in Money's view, is not what to do in the aftermath of a circumcision error. It is about the validity of feminist principles and the legitimacy of social science. And, as he sees it, the stakes are high.

&

Tea with the Queen Mum

Published in the Listener, *in January 1998, after meeting the Queen Mother at
St James's Palace the previous year.*

*W*ALTER BAGEHOT CITED THE CAPACITY OF ROYALTY to inspire awe
— and the social cohesion that resulted from this — as a major
justification for constitutional monarchy. I discovered in London last
year that the old formula still works, at least in relation to the royal
family's oldest member.

The elderly valet in the club where I was staying was explaining to
me why the advertised 'same day' laundry service would take four or
five days to return my shirts.

"You see it's Bank Holiday weekend, sir. So the staff only work part
of the day on Friday. Then they're off until Tuesday. So we couldn't get
anything back to you until Tuesday evening at the earliest, possibly
Wednesday morning . . ."

"Even if I've got a special function on Tuesday afternoon?" I pleaded.

"I'm sorry, sir, it's just not possible."

I paused for effect before playing a trump card that I would in all
probability hold only once in my life. "You see, the function's at St
James's Palace, hosted by the Queen Mother. That's why I need a dress
shirt."

The effect was as magical as anything Walter Bagehot could have envisaged. "The Queen Mother, sir? Now there's a fine lady. We've never forgotten how she turned out in the East End to encourage us during the Blitz. I'll speak to the staff, sir. I'm sure they'll make a special effort if it's for the Queen Mum." And they did. Despite Bank Holiday weekend, I got my shirt back, washed, starched and impeccably pressed.

The occasion was one of those opportunities that colonials in London find irresistible. "In the gracious presence of Her Majesty Queen Elizabeth the Queen Mother . . . to be held in the State Apartments of St James's Palace . . . lounge suit with full medals . . ."

It came about as a consequence of one of my father's naval friendships from World War II. Kevin Walton, with whom he had served on Arctic convoy escorts, had won an Albert Medal after the war by rescuing a man from a crevasse on an Antarctic glacier. In some mysterious Whitehall rationalisation, Albert Medals had subsequently been swapped for George Crosses, the highest honour conferred by the Crown on civilians for acts of "the most conspicuous courage in circumstances of extreme danger..." And every two years George Cross holders and winners of the highest military award, the Victoria Cross, gathered in London for a reunion, commemorative service and afternoon tea with the Queen Mother. Last year I joined them — not as a result of heroism, but as an honorary member of the Walton family.

Friends in London exhibited a keen interest in the forthcoming encounter with the Queen Mother, although not for any reason that Bagehot would have recognised. "Find out if the old lady's gaga," said one. "Surely she only goes through the motions with a simple script and an army of minders? Engage her in conversation. Get a response. See if there's anybody home." I undertook to carry out the mission and return with intelligence.

The service, in St Martin-in-the-Fields on Trafalgar Square, was profoundly moving — especially the sight of the VC winners, whose numbers are severely depleted by the passage of time and the Grim Reaper. (Recent acts of heroism have not replenished the ranks. VCs awarded in the Falklands war were posthumous.) Most were World War Two veterans, in wheelchairs, on crutches, stooped, wizened, reduced in physical stature by age and infirmity. But almost all exhibited flashing eyes and an alert bearing. And the small bronze cross pinned to their lapels testified that, more than half a century before, they had acted with greater regard for the welfare of their fellows than for their own safety.

Jack Hinton, New Zealand's sole-surviving VC winner, was not there. He was to die only weeks later. But George Cross holders John Gregson of Tauranga and Alfred Lowe of Auckland were, and their stories were every bit as inspirational as those of military exploits. I was introduced to Sue Ryder, now Baroness Ryder of Warsaw, widow of Leonard Cheshire VC, but a hero in her own right. It was difficult to imagine that this tiny woman had run trucks through German blockades in Eastern Europe to help supply the Polish Resistance.

After the service, we were bussed to St James's Palace at the end of the Mall. There we handed in coats, bags and cameras, and passed into a world of museum-like opulence: Italianate ceilings, wallpaper as thick as carpet, 18th and 19th century pictures looming in large frames, among them Rorke's Drift, an incident from the Zulu wars that thousands of British schoolboys have re-created in tableaux.

We were seated around a dozen tables stacked with sandwiches and cake. Next to me, to my surprise and pleasure, I found Lady S, in a wheelchair. Her husband, now deceased, had commanded a destroyer in the Battle of the Barents Sea in 1942 — an action in which Kevin Walton and my father had won Distinguished Service Crosses for extinguishing fires that threatened to destroy the vessel.

Their captain had his right eye torn out by shrapnel and was awarded the VC. As a boy at Paremata, I'd had his autographed portrait in my bedroom. Captain S, by then an admiral, had silver hair and an aristocratic bearing and looked every inch a naval hero. Now, forty years on, I was sitting alongside his widow. Again, I was moved.

Sadly, the lady's memory was all but gone. Kevin explained loudly who I was, and she professed herself delighted to meet me. Very soon, however, she was confusing me with my father and demanding to know why I wasn't wearing decorations. We went through the introductions and the story again; and again she was delighted, having no recollection of having met me minutes before.

This difficult conversation was interrupted by those, who were able, rising en masse out of respect for the Queen Mother, who had just entered the state room. In the thicket of heads and hats that surrounded us, however, we were unable to witness the royal progress. We resumed our seats in a Mexican wave when an unseen signal indicated that our hostess had taken a place at one end of the far tables.

Conversation continued. Lady S asked who we all were, and we told her. Again. Again she was delighted. Baroness Ryder, discovering that I was an historian, wanted to know who was the last monarch to live in St James's Palace. I had no idea. So I told her instead about King Tawhiao's visit to London in 1884, and King Te Rata's audience with King George V and Queen Mary in 1914. We laboured our way through high tea. And, since Lady S and I shared diabetes, I passed her the least injurious items of food.

Suddenly all those at the next table were on their feet again. The Queen Mother was on the move. We, too, rose and craned our necks for a sight of the royal personage. "There are the corgis," reported Kevin, as the excitement mounted. And so there were, two of them, running wide like fighter escorts on the flanks of a knot of people advancing towards us.

The Queen Mother hove into view in the centre of the group, a short, stoutish woman in blue pastel colours, trademark veil falling from the front of her upturned hat brim. She planted her feet wide and walked stiffly with the help of a stick. But if she was in pain, there was no sign of it on her face. She beamed and nodded to guests as she shuffled past them.

Some yards from our table, she halted. The tall gentleman from the Victoria Cross and George Cross Association made as if to wheel the group to the left towards the other side of the room. Panic! Time for the kind of rapid initiative that had brought this lot medals. "Quick," Kevin said to me, "turn Lady S around." I seized the handles of the wheelchair and spun Lady S, who was now singing "Tulips from Amsterdam", in the direction of the Queen Mother. The sudden movement caught her eye and she stopped turning away. Instead, she advanced on Lady S, gloved hand extended.

With one bound, Kevin was at her side. "This is Lady S, Ma'am. One of your former ladies-in-waiting. Her husband, as you'll know, won his VC on *Onslow*. I was there as senior engineer. And this young man" — me? Young? — "this young man all the way from New Zealand is the son of the first officer."

"Ah yes," said the Queen Mother, smiling with even greater radiance. "*Onslow*. How very nice that you've all been able to get together here." The voice was Home Counties, a little quavery but emphatic and clipped.

Then Lady S, suddenly realising whose hand she held, became instantaneously fluent and launched into a long story about a relation of hers known to the Queen Mother. The Queen Mother nodded attentively. Then she turned to Kevin and asked, "Do you think . . ." At which point Lady S managed to retrieve the hand and, with considerable lucidity and determination, told her story again.

When the second recital ended, the Queen Mother withdrew her hand and looked at me. "What part of New Zealand are you from?" I said, "The Coromandel Peninsula, Ma'am. I expect you've never heard of it." "Oh yes," she said. "I've never been there. But I've seen it from Auckland. It's got a cape named after one of the Admiralty lords, hasn't it?" (It has: Cape Colville. Not a lot of people who live there know that.)

"Have you ever been here before?" she continued. "Not to St James's, Ma'am," I said. (Extraordinary how easily one slipped into the idiom.) "But I did see you at the Auckland Domain in 1958. And my father saw you at Buckingham Palace in 1943. And my mother saw you at Newtown Park in Wellington in 1927. That's a very lengthy public career you've had." "Ah well," she said, looking pleased, "one never quite planned it that way. One just keeps going."

At which point Lady S flayed about for the royal hand and launched into her story a third time. Now the Queen Mother looked alarmed. The gentleman escort took her arm and deftly turned her towards the other side of the room. One last smile over her shoulder and she hobbled away. Our audience was over. Inevitably, there was some disappointment at the table that three people had monopolised the opportunity. "At least," a woman from California said behind me, "I got to pat a corgi. That's something to tell the folks."

What *did* one — the contagious idiom persisted — make of all this? The old lady retained her marbles, no doubt about that; and she had rather more of them than most people in the room that day. What about Bagehot's "capacity to inspire awe"?

Clearly, whatever the shortcomings of her grandchildren, the Queen Mother still exhibits that almost mystical quality. The effect of her presence on the people around us that day was dynamic. Elderly servicemen — Gurkhas, Chindits, Malays, as well as British — were electrified by her presence. The George Cross winner from Sarawak had tears in his eyes for an hour after conversation with her. And I could not but be conscious that this woman had known New Zealand prime ministers from the time of Gordon Coates and had presided over a great hui hosted by Mita Taupopoki and Apirana Ngata at Rotorua in 1927.

Seventy years later, when she could have taken refuge in deserved retirement and spent the day knitting and watching videos, here she had been instead, working the tables, pleasing the crowd, exuding what appeared to be unfeigned interest and charm in conversation after mind-numbing conversation. And all this while troubled by arthritic hips.

My republican inclinations survive undiminished. But I retain with them a vast respect for a stocky woman as old as the century who knows how to grace occasions and to give people immense pleasure. Long may she reign — or, at the very least, preside . . .

&

A Vision for the New Millennium

This essay was commissioned by the Sunday Star Times *for a millennium supplement published on 2 January 2000. Other contributors included Janet Frame, Allen Curnow, Vincent O'Sullivan and Witi Ihimaera.*

*I*N NEW ZEALAND, THE HIGHLIGHT of the first millennium of the Christian calendar was one that went unobserved in a land empty of humanity, but was seen and felt elsewhere: the Taupo eruption in the second century AD.

This cataclysm ripped a hole in the heart of the North Island, launched tsunami waves into the Pacific, and choked skies around the globe with a red dust that was recorded in China during the Later Han Dynasty and in Rome in the reign of the Emperor Commodus.

The most important events of the second millennium *were* observed. The first was the discovery of New Zealand by ancestors of the Maori at the beginning of the era, making the country the last major land mass on earth, other than Antarctica, to be occupied by humankind; and the second its rediscovery by European navigators in the 17th and 18th centuries, which led to further and far more disruptive human colonisation in the two hundred years that followed.

It is impossible, of course, to predict what will come to be seen as the most significant landmark of the third millennium. It may be another eruption that dwarfs the Taupo explosion, just as the Taupo conflagration dwarfs those that followed, such as Krakatoa's and Tarawera's. Should humankind survive another thousand years, however, I think it likely that New Zealanders would most value the fact that the country's First and Second peoples, Maori and Pakeha, achieved a harmonious accommodation in the era that followed the millennium of colonisation; and learned to live in harmony with their environment as well as with each other.

To do this, both groups and the individuals who constitute them will have to find what poet Allen Curnow called "the trick of standing upright here". Maori, I would suggest, having lost that equilibrium in the wake of European colonisation of the country, are now well on the way to regaining it. Many Pakeha, however, especially those unnerved by the spectacle of the Maori renaissance, have perhaps a further distance to travel before they accomplish a comparable sense of equipoise.

The Curnow poem, which came from a 1943 collection, *Sailing or Drowning*, was precipitated by the spectacle of an articulated skeleton of *Dinornis giganteus*, a giant moa, standing in the Canterbury Museum — what the poet referred to as a "moa on iron crutches" that exhibited an "interesting failure to adapt on islands". The poem concluded:

"Not I, some child born in a marvellous year,
"Will learn the trick of standing upright here."

From the time I first read them in adolescence, I felt that these lines spoke to me directly, for a variety of reasons. I too had been riveted by the sight of a reconstructed moa, the emu-feathered one that stood in the Dominion Farmers Institute Building in Featherston Street, Wellington, and mourned a past sacrificed to human recklessness. I too felt that I had been born in a "marvellous year", when the Second World War came to an end and servicemen returned home to construct an idyll of domestic and family bliss that the war and the Great Depression had denied them previously. Had I been born a generation earlier, I would have been part of a working-class family in the Depression years, and that would have excluded the possibility of secondary and university education. A generation later, and I would have been part of the contemporary group that enters the work force after tertiary education with an albatross of debt around its collective neck.

As to the poem's other preoccupation, the question of whether one belonged in the place of one's birth or the country of one's ancestors, that too was a resonant question. There was a flavour to my childhood years that suggested that we could have been displaced Irish. But, on the whole, I had few doubts that I belonged here — again thanks to the marvellous year of my birth. Curnow's generation, and that of my parents, were the last New Zealanders to call the United Kingdom "Home".

In another poem, *House and Land*, Curnow had written, "The spirit of exile . . . is strong in the people still"; and, "what great gloom stands in a land of settlers with never a soul at home". The Baby Boomers felt no such sense of exile. As we reached adulthood, we took it for granted that we belonged to, and identified with, the land of our birth. I came to know and love this country's history and landscape and seascape and flora and fauna in a breadth and depth that I know no other. New Zealand is part of the very marrow of my bones. And I am part of a culture that has been here long enough now to transform itself, in association with the land and the tangata whenua culture, into something that is, in effect, a second indigenous culture.

Such a degree of Pakeha identification with this land is not yet universal. Some of my Pakeha compatriots are still so far out of synchronisation with their country that they reject an indigenous name for their culture and insist on using only one — the term "New Zealander" — devised by Dutch cartographers who never even set foot here.

I was also distressed to hear the then Minister of Treaty Settlements, Sir Douglas Graham, say on one occasion that Maori had spiritual feelings for lakes and mountains and rivers that Pakeha people neither shared nor understood. He is wrong. Such a feeling among Pakeha people is now widely shared; and, as our Pakeha culture puts down even deeper roots into the soil of this country, and as those roots become more hallowed by the passage of time, those feelings will become common and more intense.

This increasingly pervasive reality cries out to be identified, acknowledged and respected. Maori people say now that *their* place as tangata whenua in Aotearoa New Zealand needs to be acknowledged and respected; and I agree. Their nearly one thousand years of occupation of this land, and the intimate relationship they have developed with it, has earned such an acknowledgment. They signed a treaty with the British Crown, protecting many of their rights; and that treaty is recognised as still having moral and judicial force.

But the very same treaty gave Pakeha people the right to be here ("tangata tiriti", as Judge Eddie Durie calls them). I would now say to

Maori that my position as a member and practitioner of the country's second indigenous culture also has a right to be acknowledged and respected. And I will not allow anyone to demean or diminish the status of my culture in the process of establishing or elevating that of Maori.

The position we must grow towards, if we are to achieve social harmony and national stability, is one of a mutuality of respect between the two major cultures. Neither side has the right to say, "I insist that you value my culture but I retain the right to revile and demean yours." That is simply a recipe for the kind of unrelenting conflict and grief that has characterised the Balkans and Northern Ireland.

Maori culture, charged by its own dynamics but helped by the resource claims made possible through the Waitangi Tribunal, has, on the whole, reasserted its mana and become strong and confident in the land in which it evolved. Pakeha people too must become strong and confident in their identity, as members of the teina or younger-sibling culture.

A confident Pakeha culture — one which knows its own history and feels positive about an allegiance to its own origins — is more likely to deliver an equable and equitable relationship with Maori. And those who respect and value their own heritage are not only happier and healthier people than those who do not. They are also equipped with the insight and compassion necessary to respect the lives and histories of their fellow citizens.

Maori and Pakeha cultures may both be extinct after the passage of another thousand years, and join the moa as the subjects of museum displays (super yachts alongside waka at Te Papa, Tupperware bowls alongside gourds). Or a volcanic eruption the size of the one that occurred eighteen hundred years ago may render the country unfit for occupation. But I hope not. As always, optimism of the will challenges pessimism of the intellect.

My vision for the future, then, is that my Pakeha brothers and sisters will achieve the same confidence and security in their identification with this land that Maori have; and that the cultures will respect and harmonise with each other. And with that object in view, I close with a millennium invocation that comes from the very heart of this country, and which I first heard from my father's Ngati Maniapoto friend, Bill Herewini:

Kia hora te marino
Kia whaka papa pounamu te moana
Kia tere te karohirohi.

May the calm be widespread
May the sea glisten like greenstone
And may the warmth of summer fall upon us all.

&

Allegiance to One's Origins: The Consequences of Belief

A paper delivered to the Sea of Faith Network Conference, "Beyond Belief — Putting Faith Into Practice", Havelock North, 8 October 2000.

THE BROAD QUERY I WANT TO RAISE IS "Who do Pakeha people believe they are? What is the nature of their culture? How does that culture relate to the land of Aotearoa New Zealand? And how does it relate to the tangata whenua culture, that of Maori?"

Depending on the *answers* to these questions, which of course are questions of belief, one then asks "What are the *consequences* of those beliefs? How might behaviour reflect them, or how *ought* it do so?" And this, I submit, puts my topic directly into the "Beyond Belief" theme which frames this gathering.

I propose addressing these questions because they have arisen from a particular journey which I have made in Aotearoa New Zealand. In the course of that journey, some odd juxtapositions have occurred, some unexpected insights been sparked, and I have witnessed a great deal of discussion, and sometimes conflict, generated by the topic.

A second reason relates to why I revised and republished last year a book I had originally written nearly two decades earlier: *Being Pakeha.* In the introduction to the new edition I said that the first book arose from what I saw twenty years ago as a need to make Maori preoccupations and expectations intelligible to Pakeha New Zealanders;

to make it clear why I believed that Maori had every right to be Maori in their own country, and to expect Pakeha to respect and support them in that mission.

Two decades on, however, at the beginning of the *twenty-first* century AD, I noted a rather different but equally pressing need: to help explain Pakeha New Zealanders to Maori and to themselves; and to do so in terms of *their* right to live in this country, practise their cultures and values and be themselves.

And I was impelled to move in this direction by a variety of stimuli, including the anguished cry of children's writer Jack Lasenby, who asked in a *Landfall* essay, "Does belief in pluralism mean one must betray one's own civilisation for another's?" And that question was provoked by a fear that he could value the restored place of Maori culture in our national life only by devaluing, or condemning, the role of his own culture, which had been that of the colonisers of the tangata whenua.

These are the circumstances, then, which conditioned my choice of topic. Let me now address that topic by saying a little more about the first version of the book called *Being Pakeha*.

Some people, some of the reviewers of the book and others who commented on it on radio and in the print media, characterised it as the work of a sickly white liberal sucking up to Maori culture and begging to be let into its inner sanctum. The grossest expression of this view came in a letter I received from a Hamilton reader who told me that I was what was known in the United States as a "nigger lover", and that I had betrayed my own culture and people.

To my mind, needless to say, this is a caricature of that book's approach and content. I had been intent on describing my experience of coming into contact with what used to be called "things Maori" — in the belief that that was a kind of encounter that would eventually be shared by all Pakeha New Zealanders; and that all Pakeha New Zealanders ought to be *prepared* for it.

But at the time I had that experience, from the mid-1960s to the early '70s, I felt very strong in my own sense of identity, as a Pakeha New Zealander with Irish-Catholic antecedents. I felt very much in accord — and still do — with both my living culture and my culture of origin. While we all, if we are healthy human beings, remain open to the influences and the richness of new experience, I was not, and am not, an empty vessel waiting to be filled up with, and consoled by, somebody else's culture.

What I did feel, however, and tried to convey in the book, was a welcome congruence of some of the inclusive qualities of tikanga Maori and taha Maori with aspects of my own Irish-Catholic experience: a love of language and eloquence; a strong sense of family; how much the function and the customs of tangihanga resembled those of the Irish wake; an easy resort to song and story to convey the substance of a culture and to express group solidarity and mutual support; an enjoyment of physical as well as emotional closeness.

This was in no way tantamount to saying I *was* Maori, or *wanted* to be Maori — because I couldn't be Maori and had no wish to be. It was rather something we all take consolation from at some stages of our lives: celebrating those things that have resonance from one culture to another — those things that remind us that, in addition to being Maori and Pakeha, male and female, gay and straight, we are also human. And there are times when we need to be reminded of that fact, and to cross the bridges to one another with which experience provides us.

I was recently made aware of this primal need to find and sustain the humanity in each one of us by something which Janet Frame said in a letter to a friend just after the death by drowning of her sister Isabel, almost ten years to the day after her older sister, Myrtle, had died the same way.

"We are such sad small people," she wrote, "standing, each alone in a circle, trying to forget that death and terror are near. But death comes, and terror comes, and then we join hands and the circle is really magic. We have the strength then to face terror and death, even to laugh and make fun of being alive, and after that even to make more music and writing and dancing. But always, deep down, we are small sad people standing humanly alone. Oh for the hands to be joined for ever and the magic circle never to be broken . . ."

I want now to turn to the subject of the nature of Pakeha culture as I perceive it; and to the question of how it relates to this land. Before I do so, however, I need to deal with definitions or descriptions of the terms I am using.

Culture, in the sense in which I use the word in this discussion, bears a close relationship to Janet Frame's "magic circle". It refers to the devices we develop to help us come to terms with the fact that we know we are alive; and we know that we are destined to die. Culture began when our ancestors started to tell stories to explain who they were and where they had come from and how they related to the world around them, seen and unseen; and to paint pictures on cave walls to illustrate the textures of those stories for the eye and the mind.

These devices in their 21st century forms can be challenging and character-building in the form of sport; they can be sheer digression in the form of entertainment (what T S Eliot was thinking of, perhaps, when he spoke of people being "distracted from distraction by distraction"); they can help to bring us into harmony with the natural world through activities such as gardening, tramping or camping; they can engage our spiritual faculties through membership of religious groups; they can have profound resonance in our consciousness and experience through the so-called high arts of music, painting and literature. Culture can, as Eliot also said, set the inner self into the most vigorous vibration; or it can simply provide the warmth of human companionship at the RSA club on a cold evening.

There are contours and textures in these activities which allow us to distinguish one form of culture from another, and to identify more closely with one kind than with another.

As Arthur Schlesinger writes, "Rhythms, patterns, continuities drift out of time past to mould the present and to colour the shape of things to come." But what they have most in common is that, at one end of the scale, they provide us with understanding of ourselves as particular people alive at particular places, at particular times; and at the other they simply distract us from realities we find too harsh to contemplate unrelievedly. Culture is, in the end, the sum total of what people do to enable themselves to cope with reality.

In using the word Pakeha, I refer to those things that relate to New Zealand but which are not specifically Maori or Pacific Island in character. I refer, in other words, to mainstream New Zealand culture — which is not unaffected by "things Maori"; but which is not in itself Maori. And I prefer to use the term Pakeha because it is *positive* (as opposed to "non-Maori"); because it is an indigenous New Zealand expression; and because the words "European" or "Caucasian" are no longer accurate or appropriate (and the word Caucasian never was).

Pakeha is not a pejorative expression. It does not mean "long pig", "white flea", "turnip", or "bugger ya" — all of which have been cited as alleged meanings by those who find the term distasteful. It almost certainly comes from the expression Pakepakeha, a reference to the white complexion of the earliest non-Maori who stepped ashore here, whose main visible distinguishing feature was that their skin was paler than that of Maori.

In identifying my own culture as Pakeha, I do so as one who has always taken for granted that I belonged in this land. And choosing a New Zealand label for that culture, one that has no significance anywhere else in the world, is a way of emphasising that fact. It's true that there was, in my childhood, a notion that we could have been displaced Irish. But that receded as I grew up. My people, predominantly remnants of the Irish diaspora, came here to a country where the first indigenous people had made a treaty with the Crown that authorised colonisation and gave us those two streams of people with rights to be here: tangata whenua, by virtue of their prior occupation, and tangata tiriti (to use Eddie Durie's characterisation of them), those who came to settle here as a result of the signing of the Treaty of Waitangi and the constitutional steps that that set in motion.

After several generations of my family's occupation of this land, my own sense of belonging to it — and hence the flavour of my own culture — includes the following ingredients: a strong relationship with the natural world intensified by living by the sea, boating, fishing, tramping and camping; an engagement with the history of the land, which began with my boyhood encounters with kainga, whaling and battle sites around Paremata Harbour; a relationship with the literature of this country, especially the writing of such people as Robin Hyde, Charles Brasch, Frank Sargeson, Eric McCormick, Keith Sinclair, James K Baxter and Janet Frame; and a relationship with Maori *people*, Maori *writing* and Maori *history*, which affects my view of all the preceding elements.

My identification with Pakeha culture is also a consequence of an accumulation of other New Zealand attitudes, values and habits which accrue to one living here like iron filings to a magnet. I am referring to such things as the rugby culture, which absorbed almost all New Zealand males of my generation and those immediately preceding it; a willingness to have a go at any kind of job opportunity that presented itself, and to learn about the job *on* the job (I recall Stephanie Dowrick saying that, in London publishing houses, an English staff member could edit a manuscript or tie up a paper parcel, whereas a New Zealander in the same office could do both); a concern for the underdog; compassion for those in need or in trouble; an unwillingness to be bullied, or to be intimidated by class or status; not undertaking to do something without seeing it through (what Dan Davin, in a very New Zealand metaphor, referred to as "a kind of power behind the scrum that was often lacking in one's more fastidious English colleagues").

Another ingredient in this equation is having New Zealand heroes and heroines, and, for me, they were such people I knew about from childhood as Cliff Porter, J T Paul, Denis Glover, Charles Upham, Suzanne Aubert, Francois Delach; and later, such figures as Robin Hyde, William Malone, Howard Kippenberger, Ormond Wilson, Frank Sargeson, E H McCormick and Janet Frame. There were also *Maori* who were part of my personal pantheon — Te Whiti O Rongomai, Te Rau-o-te-rangi, Huria Matenga, Te Puea, Sir James Henare, Whina Cooper; and, one would have to say, having access to *Maori* experience and *Maori* role models is one of the features that distinguishes Pakeha culture from its cultures of origin.

Pakeha culture shares some ingredients with its largely European cultures of origin: such as the English language, the Westminster Parliamentary system, the traditions and the conventions of the Open Society, in which every person is entitled to seek truth through a process of unfettered investigation and open disputation. But the forms and the proportions in which those imported ingredients have coalesced in New Zealand has made them somewhat different in character from their antecedents, and hence characteristic of Pakeha culture rather than of European culture.

If anyone doubts this, they have only to travel abroad, to do the much-valued 'OE', to discover that this is so. And what one discovers is that one may feel a sense of affinity in places such as England, or (in my case) Ireland, or Scotland. But that sense of affinity is not the same as feeling at home. In fact no sooner is one separated for a substantial length of time from New Zealand voices, viewpoints or even the sense of humour, than one misses them, and knows oneself to be from and of New Zealand, and not from and of any other place on earth.

Travel overseas at the age of thirty confirmed and emphasised for me that it is *New Zealand* and its experience and traditions, Maori and Pakeha, that is in my bones; and that there is no other part of the globe in which I would want to live or could live with the same sense of belonging and enrichment.

Among the subsequent experiences that have sharpened that feeling for me are being informed by members of the Aahi Kaa group that I was in fact a tau iwi or foreigner in this land; and, just as offensively, listening to Cabinet Minister Doug Graham say that Maori people had spiritual feelings for lakes, mountains and rivers, and that Pakeha people did not. Doug Graham might not have those feelings, but I and my family have them, as have the thousands of other Pakeha people I have encountered in four decades of walking, tramping and camping on this beautiful land; and doing their best to preserve the contours and the character of Papa-tua-nuku from a variety of commercial interests which have sought to destroy that character by ill-considered development projects.

It is for all these reasons that I would say now what I did not go as far as to say two decades ago: that Pakeha culture can no longer be considered an imported culture; it has now been here long enough, in interaction with the land and the tangata whenua, to be considered a *second indigenous culture*. And it has become indigenous in the same way that East Polynesian culture became Maori culture in New Zealand: by turning the attention of migrants away from their land and culture of origin, and focusing their sense of commitment to this land.

Just one indication of how far Pakeha have moved in this direction in the course of two generations can be gauged from the New Zealand response to the Second World War. In 1939 a New Zealand Prime Minister could say, "Where Britain goes, we go; where she stands, we stand..." And one hundred and five thousand New Zealanders served abroad in response to that call to defend Britain, Europe and something called the British Empire. That cannot happen, and won't ever happen, in the future. New Zealanders would only ever take up arms again on that scale to defend New Zealand.

In the new edition of *Being Pakeha*, I go on to say that, as another indication of how far Pakeha culture has become indigenous, it is only right to see the macrocarpa and the wooden church as being as much emblematic of the New Zealand landscape and human occupation of it as the meeting house and the cabbage tree.

In saying this, and in saying what preceded this, I am in no way taking anything away from the position of Maori as tangata whenua, the nation's First Culture. Maori were, are and will remain the tuakana or senior sibling in our whanau relationship with the land, with each other, and with the outside world. They remain the people who, by virtue of being here first, signed with the Crown a treaty that is still recognised as having moral and judicial force.

But having said that, I will not willingly allow anybody to demean or diminish the status of *my* culture in the process of establishing or elevating that of Maori. And that brings me to the relevance of the Jack Lasenby quotation I mentioned earlier. There are several grounds for resisting the notion that respect for Maori implies disrespect for one's own heritage, if that heritage can be seen to have disadvantaged Maori.

One is that I don't believe in the Old Testament notion that the sins of the fathers are to be visited on successive generations. That is a prescription for the kind of payback culture that has crippled such places as the Balkans and Northern Ireland for centuries. Further, if one accepted such a principle, it would also be a recipe for continued conflict between Maori and Maori as a consequence of the musket wars of the early 19th century. Then there are the potentially difficult implications for those who are both Maori *and* Pakeha in descent.

It is in that latter circumstance, however, that we have a precedent for a way forward and out of a culture of revenge. In the pre-musket, pre-contact years, when Maori iwi or hapu fought other iwi or hapu and one side achieved clear dominance, the descendants of both victor and vanquished were married, so that their descendants could whakapapa back to both sides. And *that* was a prescription for ending the distinction between victor and vanquished and thus removing grounds for future conflict. In this way did Ngati Mamoe absorb Waitaha in the South Island; and then were themselves absorbed by Ngai Tahu; and in this way, too, most Ngai Tahu descendants now trace their descent from all three iwi.

The "sins of the fathers" model also loses validity if one takes it literally, case by case. When North Island Maori were being attacked by Imperial and then colonial government forces in the middle of the 19th century, *my* immediate ancestors were grappling with the effects of the Irish famines; and my Tierney grandmother always asserted that we, with four hundred years of oppression of our language, our culture and our faith, had more reason to hate the English than those who had survived the decidedly more mild consequences of 19th century colonisation.

That is not to say that one should devalue or underestimate the effect on Maori of the British colonisation of Aotearoa. I have researched and documented the pain and the grief of that process in half a dozen books; and done as much as I can to make the negative effects of that colonisation visible to my Pakeha brothers and sisters; and argued forcefully that it created imbalances of opportunity in our national life that can and ought to be compensated for and remedied. Which is one reason that I am fully supportive of the Treaty-based claims process and applaud the fact that it returns economic and social resources to people who had had those things illegally or unethically taken from them.

But that is not the same as saying that Maori people or Maori culture are ethically or morally *superior* to Pakeha because of the European colonisation of New Zealand. That is a notion I wholly reject. The process of colonisation is about the application of power on the part of those who have it, onto those who do not. And it is almost inevitably corrupting, as Lord Acton reminded us when speaking of the absolute variety. And it brings with it, as part of its baggage, notions of racial and cultural superiority.

Note that I say that it is the *process* that brings these things, not simply *people* of one kind of ethnic background or another. In pre-European contact days, tribal Maori interacted only with each other. And those people, Nga Iwi o te Motu, while there were small variations in their language and kawa, recognised a broad tikanga that was intelligible to and accepted by people from Te Rerenga Wairua in the north to Rakiura in the south.

In the first half of the 19th century, however, individual iwi considered carrying their martial culture beyond the shores of New Zealand. At least three expeditions of conquest were planned: to Samoa, to Norfolk Island, and to the Chatham Islands, which did not become part of New Zealand until 1842. All these proposed expeditions were dependent on finding transport to those places: and that meant finding a European ship's captain whose vessel was available for charter; or it meant Maori commandeering a vessel for the purpose.

In the event, there were no expeditions to Norfolk Island or to Samoa because the necessary transport was not secured. But there *was* an invasion of the Chathams Islands. Two Taranaki tribes then based in Wellington, Ngati Tama and Ngati Mutunga Ki Poneke, hijacked a European vessel in 1835 and had themselves — a total of nine hundred people — delivered to Chatham Islands. There they takahi'd or walked the land to claim it; ritually killed around three hundred Chatham Moriori out of a total of around sixteen hundred, then enslaved the survivors — separating husbands from wives, parents from children, forbidding them to speak their own language or practise their own customs, and forcing them to violate the tapus of their culture, whose mana was based on the rejection of violence.

Was this a superior form of colonisation to that imposed by Europeans on Maori? Did it respect the dignity and customs of the colonised? Did it acknowledge the mana whenua of the tchakat henu or indigenous people of the Chathams? It did not. It was what might now be called an exercise in ethnic cleansing. When Bishop Selwyn arrived in the islands in 1848, it was to discover that the Maori called Moriori "Paraiwhara" or "Blackfellas"; and it was to report that the Moriori population continued to decline at a suicidal rate as a consequence of kongenge or despair. Moriori slaves were not released and New Zealand law was not established on the islands until 1862, twenty years after they had become part of New Zealand. And it is that twenty years of neglect of fiduciary duty on the part of the Crown that is the basis for the Moriori claim to the Waitangi Tribunal, heard in 1994, but still not reported upon.

The point in raising the Chathams experience is not to use it as a stick with which to beat Maori — especially in view of what I have been saying about not visiting the sins of the fathers, or mothers, onto subsequent generations. I draw attention to it in the spirit of an historian who says, Take care. The evidence of history is unanimous on only one point. It shows us that no race or culture is inherently superior or inferior to another; and we all have skeletons in our ancestral closets that represent instances of behaviour of which we cannot be wholly proud by today's standards of ethics and morality.

There is another issue which falls within the context of Jack Lasenby's quote about the respective balance between valuing and devaluing our major cultures. And it is exemplified most emphatically, I believe, by the behaviour of our National Museum, Te Papa.

This excellent institution made an early decision to recognise and provide access to Matauranga Maori — Maori systems of knowledge — alongside Western scholarly conventions; and by so doing to provide the country's indigenous and Pacific cultures with the major say in how their cultures would be presented in the museum's displays. Thus notices in the museum ask visitors to respect the values and protocols arising out of those cultures. Thus the same visitors are asked to remove their shoes before entering the meeting house Te Hau Ki Tauranga. And thus, at the request of New Zealand Samoans, Tongans and other Polynesians, pictures of bare-breasted women taken by European photographers in the 19th and early 20th centuries were not hung in Te Papa's Pacific section, because such images are offensive to the evangelical-Christian mores of the descendants of those same women.

So far so good. I have no grounds for wanting to challenge such a policy. But I am made uneasy by the fact that when an issue arose about the mores and sensibilities of a section of our Pakeha culture, Christians who venerated the Mother of Christ every bit as reverentially as Poverty Bay Maori venerated the carvings in Te Hau Ki Tautanga, there was no sign of mutuality of respect. The Virgin in a Condom was allowed to remain on display regardless of the offence that it gave. I was made even more uneasy when, at the very same time, the Waikato Museum of Arts and History decided to withdraw a Dick Frizzell exhibition on the ground that moko on the face of a caricatured Four Square grocer gave offence to Tainui Maori. The message that emerged from the exact conjunction of both episodes was that tangata whenua culture is to be respected by the institutions responsible for New Zealand art and ethnology; but Pakeha culture, our second indigenous culture, is not.

There was one further episode involving Te Papa that seemed to reinforce this message. Four professional historians (I was not one of them) wrote last year to Te Papa's chief executive officer, Cheryl Sotheran, complaining that the Moriori exhibit made no mention of the Maori invasion of the Chathams, to which I have already referred. Defending Te Papa's representation of Moriori history, the museum's manager of research went on to the *Holmes* television programme to say that "a revelation of the truth [in this matter] would constitute a return to a view of history which has overtones of racism."

Again, I was left feeling uncomfortable. This defence implied that aspects of the past ought to be suppressed if they gave comfort to rednecks. That, I would argue, is not a sound ground for misrepresenting history. And I'm not sure that I can think of *any* justifiable reason for doing so. The only healthy way to deal with the past, and to understand it, is to have all the relevant incidents and episodes on the table and to be even-handed in the manner in which we deal with them.

This last episode raises the issue of whether or not, in an effort to compensate Maori for past injustices and misrepresentations, some of us are now presenting history slanted in such a way as to make Maori history and behaviour appear more virtuous than the behaviour and performance of non-Maori.

The Maori historian Buddy Mikaere has referred to a tendency on the part of Pakeha historians to depict Maori as, invariably, deeply spiritual beings who only ever act on the basis of high-minded principles; and Pakeha as unprincipled rogues or fools whose behaviour is always motivated by racial arrogance, greed and self-interest.

Mikaere made these comments with specific reference to *The Story of New Zealand* by Judith Bassett, Keith Sinclair and Marcia Stenson. But the imprint of the approach to history he identifies can be found in Anne Salmond's book, *Two Worlds, First Meetings Between Maori and Europeans 1642-1772* (though interestingly enough not in its sequel, *Between Two Worlds*). It rests heavily on James Belich's series of television documentaries on the New Zealand Wars. And it is there in Fergus Clunie's recent writings on missionary activity in and around the Bay of Islands.

In the first instance, that of Anne Salmond, it is revealed in a determination to expose the more brutal features of 17th and 18th century European society without acknowledging comparable behaviour by Maori; and to judge every aspect of European activity in New Zealand in the harshest light, and every manifestation of Maori behaviour in the most benevolent and positive way.

Belich's documentaries highlight behaviour of the nincompoop variety, whilst portraying Maori as almost always making decisions that were admirable and strategically sound. And Fergus Clunie sees early missionary actions as being designed not to give Maori the benefit of European technology in such areas as food production and house construction, but solely to make Maori dependent on the technology with a view to advancing the process of colonisation and parting them from their land.

It is true, as Belich remarks, that all the encounters referred to in each of these books result from European intrusions into a previously discreet indigenous culture; and that consequently, from a post-colonial perspective, Maori in the 18th and 19th century can be seen as always occupying the moral high ground, just as Moriori do in the context of their experience of colonisation. But it is also true, as Mikaere points out, that Maori too sometimes acted precipitately, unwisely, injudiciously; and that Maori historical narratives about themselves are as replete with fools and clowns and villains as they are with heroes and heroines.

One of the features that has always characterised the writing of history is an impulse to restore balance after an interval of perceived *imbalance*. Hence, like the workings of a clock, the forward motion of history is often generated by pendulum swings. And the examples of imbalance which I have offered are themselves the consequence of previous imbalances: Salmond's against a former inability or unwillingness to perceive the process of cultural encounter from Maori perspectives; Belich's against a tradition of military history that was both racially arrogant and culturally chauvinistic; and Clunie's against a literature on missionary endeavour whose major distinguishing characteristic was filial piety.

Having noted that, however, I would go on to say that the kinds of history that portray Maori as acting only with nobility, and Pakeha acting only with malice and self-interest, are as patronising and as offensive as an earlier generation of historical narratives which either ignored the Maori role in the national equation or wrote off Maori strategies as the ineffective antics of a savage people.

Idealisation of Maori behaviour also builds up a paradigm in which it becomes difficult to accommodate other episodes in New Zealand history, such as the periodic cruelty of Maori to other Maori. Ultimately, historians have a responsibility to reflect *all* the variegations of human behaviour in these islands, to follow evidence wherever it leads, and not to write narratives that simply caricature one side or another.

Let me now try to steer this discussion towards some kind of conclusion.

What I am saying in summary about recognising the indigenising of Pakeha culture is also part of saying that there has to be a mutual acknowledgment and a mutuality of respect between our two cultures. No side is entitled to say, "I insist that you respect my culture but I reserve the right to revile and demean yours." That is simply a recipe for unrelenting social disharmony and for violence. Nor should historians mistakenly try to raise the mana and the esteem of Maori culture by idealising Maori life and caricaturing that of non-Maori.

I would also argue that a strong and confident Pakeha culture — one that actually knows its own history and feels positive about allegiance to its own origins — is more likely to deliver an equable and more equitable relationship with Maori. The people who rant and rave about Maori regaining lost ground at the *expense* of Pakeha, and who characterise the Treaty-based claims process as a form of apartheid, such as members of the One New Zealand Foundation, are for the most part people whose own cultural position is insecure. By contrast, it was no surprise to me that some of the conservatives who embraced the Maori cultural and economic revival with most enthusiasm, and helped give it further momentum, were the likes of Peter Elworthy, Doug Graham and Jim Bolger — Pakeha people who know and feel positive about their own history.

In saying what I have about Pakeha culture, about its right to be here, to belong, and to carry indigenous status, I seek to do two things: one is to reflect and articulate a reality that is evolving but not always acknowledged; the other is to accompany my Pakeha brothers and sisters towards a similar degree of confidence and security in their identification with this land as Maori have.

And I seek to do this without guilt, and without apology.

&

The Historian and Heritage Issues

A talk given to the Waikato branch of the Historic Places Trust in August 1993.
It was an attempt to put issues of historical heritage in the context of conservation.

I'M A LITTLE BIT INTIMIDATED by this talk's title, which was given to me. I find I can't really philosophise or pontificate about "*the*" historian and heritage issues. To do so would be to commit an army of fellow professionals to viewpoints that I can not be absolutely confident that they share. To avoid that, and to avoid any criticisms that I am being presumptuous, I shall adopt the less cosmic viewpoint of "this" historian and heritage issues.

Speaking for myself, then, I can say that historical and heritage issues have always been inextricably linked (and I am using the word "heritage" in its now widely accepted sense of evidence of the past that is worthy of preservation). There are professional reasons why I should view things in this manner. But there are also personal ones. And I'll begin, if I may, with a slice of autobiography, to help explain the development of my own perspectives.

As some of you may know from reading my books, I grew up on the Pauatahanui arm of the Porirua estuary in the early 1950s. I woke each morning with the windows open — a fetish of my mother's — and my first experience of every day was the smell of flowers and fruit, or of rain on earth, that came to me from the garden into which my bedroom projected. I frequently got up before dawn to fish, and watched the sun come up over the water, an exquisite experience I describe in *Being Pakeha*.

This routine, along with weekend excursions into the bush below Paekakariki Hill, or walking around the rocks from Titahi Bay to Kaumanga, boiling the billy and cooking sausages on driftwood fires as we went — all this contributed to what I would now recognise as my earliest spiritual feelings: a knowledge that I was part of nature and nature was part of me. I felt at ease in a boat, trees and birds were companionable presences, the cry of the oyster catcher was the last thing I heard at night as I fell asleep.

Parallel with the unconscious development of that cosmology was the growth of another. In that neighbourhood we were surrounded by evidence of a thousand years of human habitation: remnants of moa hunter camp sites in the dunes, traces of pa and middens around the harbour, whale ribs and vertebrae in the vicinity of what had been Thom's whaling station, the stone remains of Fort Paremata, erected at the mouth of the harbour in 1846 to intimidate Ngati Toa, and the little wooden church where we worshipped each Sunday, surrounded by macrocarpa and cabbage trees and built by Irishmen given land at Pauatahanui in return for service in the New Zealand Wars.

These relics and structures gave me a strong sense that the past was close to the present and connected to it, the two dimensions rubbing against each other to produce a frisson that animated everything one saw and felt in such a place. And this in turn merged with my love of books to produce a passionate interest in history. I've also described in *Being Pakeha* the thrill I felt as a ten-year-old when I discovered that James Cowan's *The New Zealand Wars* contained a detailed account of what had happened militarily in the neighbourhood in 1845:

"The book included maps, photographs and descriptions of combat that enabled me to pinpoint and stand on each site, and once standing there, to imagine that I was experiencing what had happened there . . . I lay in the earthworks behind the Anglican Church which had been built over Rangihaeata's pa . . . climbed Battle Hill to find the Maori rifle pits, and the graves of Imperial troops killed fighting there. These experiences made history come alive for me. I *felt* the presence of people who had gone before. I saw them in a kind of Arthurian world that was not in Camelot but (literally) on my own doorstep."

I didn't know it at the time, but this was remarkably similar to the childhood experiences of James Cowan, who grew up near Rangiaowhia, close to the sites of the Waikato Wars. Only he didn't have a volume of *The New Zealand Wars* as a guidebook. He spoke of the survivors of the battles themselves.

Intense childhood experiences leave an imprint on the adult psyche: and these ones have on mine. I am conscious wherever I go now of the resonance — the historical echo — that calls back to us from our landscape: what James K Baxter referred to as "the song of Tangaroa from a thousand beaches, the sound of wind among the green volcanoes". Wherever I go in this country I look for the evidence of people who were here before us: the contours of fortified pa, the middens in the dunes, the wooden Gothic churches that are our one memorable contribution to world architecture. All these things continue to interest me, and to comfort me. They are a large part of what makes me feel connected to these islands and to their communities.

They also, of course, reveal traits which make historians sometimes anathema to city planners and property developers. In the minds of *these* people, historians ought not to be involved in making decisions on heritage issues, because they tend to be interested in the past for its own sake and on its own terms, regardless of its relevance to the present.

The other accusation one hears about historians is that they are heavily prone to nostalgia — to living happily in their reconstructed pasts as one might in another country; and — in the process — to losing track of what is going on around them in the real world. According to this view, historians emerge from their studies — or from archives, libraries and lecture theatres — blinking and confused, like a possum caught suddenly in car headlights.

It is asserted that as historians become older, indeed — not to put too fine a point on it — as they become downright elderly, often prematurely, they are acutely subject to a world view described by an English writer:

"The summers get worse, the music noisier and more senseless, the buildings uglier, the roads more congested, the public transport slower and dirtier, the government sillier and the news more depressing. Good things, glow worms, fantails, accessible forests, good fish and chip shops and girls who enjoy being called beautiful, are slowly withdrawn. The process is possibly a merciful one: because when one comes to the end of one's allotted span in a world so remote from that in which one grew up, such a person is quite content to depart."

To which I could add, as a corollary: in a world of constant and unnecessary change, the only truly happy historian is a dead one.

All this, of course, is a caricature. But a caricature with an element of truth. What the historian *is* inclined to do, and is often very well equipped to do, is act as an advocate for the past, for people and for things no longer able to speak for themselves, except through the mouths of historians, and their readers, who hear and transmit the messages that the past sends to posterity.

Hence they may say: "*These* are the stories we need to retain in the collective memory, to recall who we are and where we come from; *these* are the events which have spawned the cultures and the communities to which we now belong; and *these* are the houses and buildings we need to preserve in order to see evidence of the umbilical cord that connects us to our history."

I like that metaphor of the umbilical cord. Because umbilical cords not only link offspring to a maternal parent, they also nourish and enrich and ensure a life and a future. And those are precisely the things that history does for a community.

History links us to our pasts, not only in relation to the literal processes of causes and effects — how we physically came to be where we are now and not somewhere else; but also in the sense of *comprehending* the present and giving us the feeling that we do indeed belong where we are.

For most of us, there is no doubt that we feel richer and more secure if we grow up with the *evidence* of our history around us. If we are fortunate enough to grow up, for example, within sight and sound of our parents and grandparents, and the homes in which we were raised, and the churches in which we were christened, and from which we buried our loved ones. And if we go through life with the reassuring presence of reference points in our landscapes: streets that we know and recognise; public buildings that have been there all our lives; beaches, forests and picnic spots which don't change, though we do.

Now I appreciate that there is a solid dollop of romanticism in such a view. The physical and natural world *does* change; landscapes change; cityscapes change; people move out of their homeplaces and deposit themselves around the globe. Change is the pulse of life on earth and is unavoidable. But the point I am making is that the very rate and pace of change makes it even more imperative that we all — as individuals and communities — get to retain some of those personal and communal reference points of which I was speaking. Because it is those things that will help us come to terms with change without losing our bearings and our equilibrium and our sense of identity and ultimately our psychic and emotional and physical health.

I am reminded of something Edmund Burke said about the fear of humankind, that they may be little more than "flies of a summer" — here today in profusion, buzzing about and making a great deal of noise, and gone tomorrow. One of the most important things that makes us feel less like flies of a summer, I think, that makes us feel that we belong to places and are part of larger continuities than simply our own individual lives, is seeing some evidence of our personal and communal past around us as we grow up and — ultimately — grow old.

In addition to the evidence of my own experience, one of the factors that has brought me forcibly to such a conclusion has been observation of and participation in the lives of Maori friends and acquaintances. I think of the strong sense of identity and confidence felt and displayed by those I know who are connected with particular places, particular iwi, particular marae; people who — regardless of what part of the country or world they live in now, return to a meeting house that is their own to resolve family and tribal matters, and to bury their dead in urupa where parents, grandparents and great-grandparents lie.

And I think conversely of Maori I know for whom that umbilical connection had been broken; and who were directionless, discontented, resentful, angry and anti-social — and anti-Pakeha — without it. And I have seen the lives of some such people transformed in their adulthood, sometimes in their advanced adulthood, by a reconnection with those whanau, iwi and marae links.

Again, I don't want to seem romantic about such things. Not all Maori are going to succeed in establishing such associations; and even fewer Pakeha New Zealanders have access to a comparable ready-made and still-intact heritage in the worlds in which they live.

What I *am* saying is that there is a danger if we live in communities that are forever shedding old skins and making — one can't even call it "growing" — new ones; forever pulling down old houses and old buildings, and then even more rapidly pulling down the new ones too, constantly altering the appearance of the landscapes and cityscapes about us. That danger is that there is more likelihood that an increasing number of our citizens will grow up rootless, feeling *emotionally* insecure, in spite of the fact that they may be financially secure. And if the emotional *and* financial insecurity coincide, the social cocktail is a lethal one.

The end point of such a process is that people *will* feel like flies of a summer, and will become restless and rootless and feel little commitment or loyalty to the places in which they live and the people among whom they live. And this is what we risk, I believe, if we continually destroy evidence of that personal and community history; because by doing that, we are erasing the reference points by which people *recognise* their community and feel that their present is connected to a past.

If people don't feel that they *have* a past, that they live only in some kind of sensation-dominated continuous present, then it is more difficult for them to believe that they have a future. And if they don't feel that they have a future and a posterity to which they in turn are contributing, then it is far less likely that they will live their lives as socially responsible citizenry.

And the consequences I am speaking of here are not simply of the kinds of vandalism wreaked by juvenile delinquents who smash telephones, spraypaint slogans and uproot saplings. I have in mind, too, the vandalism of those whom Jonathan Raban calls "the barbarians of the new": those who believe that the rural and natural resources of our land exist solely for the purpose of rapid, short-term exploitation and gratification; those who see an estuary only as an unrealised marina, or a stand of mature rimu as so many superfeet of timber, or a Victorian building as an obstacle to a far more lucrative tower block.

That's about all I want to say for the moment. But, so as not to end on too much of an apocalyptic note, I want to quote from Gordon Stephenson's excellent introduction to the draft *Conservation Management Strategy* for the Waikato conservancy. This document has been prepared by the Department of Conservation and the Waikato Conservation Board, of which Gordon is chairman, and it will be released for public discussion and comment at the end of this year (1993). I commend it for it reflects many of the attitudes and perspectives that I've been trying to clarify.

"We have all come", Gordon Stephenson writes, "from a long ancestral journey from the past: from the roots of all life through to the complexities of today. We carry within ourselves reminders of those origins. Yet for all our intellect and sophistication, we are as yet unable to understand in full even the simplest processes of the natural world.

"The air we breathe, the water we drink, the soils whence comes our nourishment, the land which supports us, and the sea which washes our shores and ultimately sources all life: all these can maintain their integrity without us; but we can't maintain ours without them, and all of them suffer if we are careless in our activities. It is in our interests to take great care of this breast of nature which succours us. We are all too frequently guilty of violations against the very processes which can ensure our survival.

"As with our natural heritage, so with our cultures. To lose our spiritual and cultural links with the past is to deprive ourselves of understanding of ourselves. That richness of life derives from the myriad influences that come from our histories, our languages, our taonga, waahi tapu, artefacts, historic sites, and our customary ways and attitudes. There has to be a commitment to the guardianship of these things, which orient us to our past, and to our present."

&

A Fraction Too Much Fiction?

This paper was delivered as the Beaglehole Lecture at the New Zealand Historical Association conference at the University of Waikato, in December 1999. It provoked a walkout on the part of some Maori present. Tom Roa, a history and Maori studies lecturer, told National Radio's Mana News that he had objected to an excerpt read out from an undergraduate essay "which provoked sniggers in the audience, which I did not appreciate at all".

ALL PROFESSIONALS INVOLVED in the writing of New Zealand history need to be scrupulous about the application of scholarly standards and ensure that their work is characterised by accuracy, precision, balance and clarity.

If this prescription is true for historians in general, it is even more imperative for those involved in the writing of Maori history, for at least two reasons.

One is that Maori history is frequently cited in the claims process and is therefore susceptible to being used or condemned as propaganda. The other is that some of our compatriots, such as members of the One New Zealand Foundation, frequently allege that Maori history is sanitised in an effort to make Maori behaviour seem more virtuous than the behaviour and performance of non-Maori. How, then, in the light of these concerns, have writers of Maori history fared in recent years?

On the whole, I would have to say very well. The best of this writing, as seen, for example in the essays in *The Dictionary of New Zealand Biography* or in Judith Binney's magisterial biography of Te Kooti Arikirangi Te Turuki, is as accomplished and as admirable as anything written anywhere in the world.

Much valuable and high-quality research, yet to be published, is being quietly carried out by graduate and post-graduate students in our universities. But outside these categories of historical activity one does occasionally encounter the commission of those old sins of inaccuracy and anachronism.

One source of such lapse, a trivial one, was an issue *of People's History*, the newsletter of the Historical Branch of the Department of Internal Affairs. This described a stern and dignified figure in a 1933 photograph as 'Te Arikinui, King Koroki'. And Koroki was, of course, the fifth Maori King and father of the present Queen, Te Atairangikaahu.

What he was not, however, was 'Te Arikinui'. This Polynesian title was coined and applied to the leader of the Kingitanga by Alex McKay, successfully secretary to Princess Te Puea and then Dame Te Ata. And he coined it in 1966 as an alternative to 'Kuini', which some non-Tainui Maori— possibly the majority— found offensive.

A second and more serious example comes from the otherwise admirable *New Zealand Historical Atlas*. It is the identification of some 19th and early 20th-century Maori place names as tupuna or ancestral names.

The most notable in this category are those that liken geographical features to the anatomy of Maui's fish. Te Ika-a-Maui was the most common pre-European name for the North Island. But the embellishments — likening Wellington Harbour to the mouth (Te Upoko-o-te-Ika), Taranaki and East Cape to the fins, Hawke's Bay to the fishhook and Northland to the tail — date from the period in which Maori recognised from European maps just how fishlike the shape of the island was as a whole.

The question has been debated many times by Maori; and scholars such as Te Kani Te Ua objected to the identification of such names as 'tupuna' ones. To say this is not to suggest that Maori culture ought to remain static, or that the names have any less significance to Maori because they were coined in post contact times. It is simply to argue that their origin ought to be identified accurately.

There is a plethora of other examples of this kind. Throughout the country, constructs devised, absolutely legitimately, to analyse and codify aspects of Maori thought or custom — such as Mason Durie's 'taha hinengaro' for mental health and 'taha tinana' for physical health, or 'kaitiakitanga' for responsibility for care of the environment — these are now being preached and taught as if they were the actual terms and concepts used by ancestors.

So is Henry Williams' 'tino rangatiratanga' for chiefly authority or, more latterly, sovereignty, and the Maori Language Commission's 'taiapure' for a category of marine reserve.

This whole process has an English language equivalent in the insistence of a Maori actress in a recent education video on the Treaty of Waitangi that her ancestors viewed the document as a 'partnership' between Maori and Crown — whereas an historian would be inclined to point out that the word 'partnership' did not appear in Maori or Pakeha analyses of the Treaty until the early 1980s.

Do such stumbles matter? They do in a context of historiography, if words such as accuracy and precision are seen to have continuing meaning and relevance. To accept the implied corollary — that accuracy is of consequence in a Pakeha context but not in a Maori one — is to demean Maori scholarship and suggest that it is insufficiently important to be governed by rigorous standards.

The most serious current misrepresentation of tangata whenua culture is the proposition that the earliest settlers in this country were a pre-Maori people known as Waitaha, and that they arrived more than two thousand years ahead of the ancestors of the Maori.

This hypothesis, which Atholl Anderson calls "the latest mutation in a virulent myth", is not being promoted by professional historians (indeed, people such as Anderson, Te Maire Tau and Tipene O'Regan have already demolished it). But it is being promoted and popularised by mainstream media, and I feel that historians have been insufficiently active in challenging it in these same media.

In brief, the "virulent myth" of which the Waitaha hypothesis is a mutation is that of the pre-Maori Moriori, who were supposedly defeated on the New Zealand mainland and driven off to the Chatham Islands by the more intelligent and more vigorous Maori who arrived in the Great Fleet of 1350. This story, as we now know from the work of David Simmons and others, was the product of a dismembering of Maori tribal traditions and a cobbling together of synthetic narratives by the likes of Stephenson Percy Smith and Elsdon Best. It has taken more than half a century to erase it from the school curriculum. And no sooner has it been erased, than another story, equally spurious, has begun to take its place.

It is the creation of Pakeha geographer Barry Brailsford, two Maori, one of Taranaki and the other of Ngapuhi descent, and a reverential band of Maori and Pakeha supporters. They claim to have had access to the teachings of the "Elders of the Ancient Nation of Waitaha".

These teachings turn out to be New Age truisms soaked in Maori mysticism— information which had, supposedly, been "hidden in the land, in the trees and in the stones".

Despite their inability to pass any tests, Maori or Pakeha, as to veracity and authenticity, these so-called teachings were published in 1995 as *Song of Waitaha, the Histories of a Nation*. Scandalously, the publication was supported by the Ministry of Education, the Christchurch College of Education, Creative New Zealand, and — for some unfathomable reason — Toyota New Zealand.

Clearly, Brailsford and his disciples feared the possibility that their book might be reviewed by people with a professional knowledge of history. And so they took a step thus far unprecedented in New Zealand publishing. In place of the conventional rubric saying that "no part of this book may be reproduced apart from any fair dealing for the purpose of private study, research, criticism or review", they printed instead a stern warning:

"In taking the unprecedented step of allowing the knowledge of the ancestors to be written for the first time, the Elders of Waitaha ask that the words, illustrations and maps shared here be respected as the sacred taonga of their people, their children, and their children's children.

"To protect the wisdom of the past, and to allow it to travel truly into the future, they place a rahui on all contained within these pages . . . [No] part of this publication may be reproduced . . . in any form . . . without the prior written permission of Ngati Kowhai o Waitaha."

Oddly, or perhaps not so oddly, "Ngati Kowhai o Waitaha" were not identified in the book, nor were the "Elders of the Ancient Nation of Waitaha".

A further series of problems relating to historical representation may arise when traditional Maori forms of scholarship, usually grouped under the heading of Matauranga Maori, do not easily harmonise with the conventions of Western scholarship.

One manifestation of such conflict may appear when what is written in a textbook or taught in the classroom appears to conflict with what the "old people" said or say.

And, because of the weight and emphasis which Maori culture gives to veneration of kuia and koroua and tupuna, the inclination of the student is often to place more reliance on whanau or hapu sources of information than on textbooks or lectures.

I had an example of such conflict in the course of teaching a New Zealand history course at this university. One student wrote in an examination paper:

"Though you . . . have taught that Maori were migrants to this country, I and my iwi do not accept your bullshit. According to my tipuna my nation were always here and no amount of talking or writing or publication on your part is going to convince me otherwise."

I don't offer that quotation to ridicule the student concerned, I do it to demonstrate the difficulty that occurs when fundamentalist beliefs come up against both the conventions and the findings of scholarship. And the case I've cited is little different from that of the Christian student who believes in the literal truth of Genesis and studies biology or palaeontology, or the Mormon student exposed to lectures on American history.

Without invalidating the belief systems of students, whether they have an ethnological or religious base or a mixture of both, we have to, as teachers or writers, persuade them to put those systems to one side when they enter the academy and take up the tools and methodology of scholarship.

The most dramatic recent example of an apparent clash between Matauranga Maori and Western scholarship, however, arises from a series of decisions taken by Te Papa, our national museum.

This institution made an early decision to recognise and provide access to Matauranga Maori alongside Western systems of knowledge, and by so doing to provide the country's indigenous and Pacific cultures with the major say in how their cultures would be presented in the museum's exhibits and displays.

This eminently worthwhile aim, however, led to a dispute on the question of how Moriori culture and history was or should be represented in the museums.

It came to light as a result of what has come to be called the 'Four Professors' Letter', addressed to the museum's chief executive, Cheryl Sotheran, in April 1999 and signed by Bill Oliver, Peter Munz, Miles Fairburn and the late David Hamer. It read in part:

"It is our duty as historians to draw attention to the fact that the standards of research in your museum are inadequate. As an example, the exhibit displaying the life and culture of the first Chatham Islanders distorts the truth by omitting all mention of the 1835 massacre of these islanders by invading Maori tribes - an early instance of ethnic cleansing.

"The exhibit does point out that these people had committed themselves to keeping peace with each other and had renounced violence. But it does not go on to note that this commitment was exploited by the Maori who massacred them.

"The truth of this event is not in question . . . and its relevance to contemporary affairs in the Balkans and in Rwanda is painfully obvious.

"Your museum is not obliged to deal with the past of the Chatham Island. But if it does, it is obliged to do so truthfully."

The letter went on to say that the museum's manager of research, Ken Gorbey, when challenged on the Holmes television programme in March, had defended the omission on the ground that "a revelation of the truth would constitute a return to a view of history which has overtones of racism". According to the historians, this was tantamount to saying that "it was 'racist' to reveal truths which show Maori in a bad light."

I haven't seen Cheryl Sotheran's reply to this letter. But the publicity generated by its leaking revealed that the situation was more complicated than the professors knew. It transpired that Te Papa's decision to represent Moriori history and culture in the manner complained of had been made in association with Te Iwi Moriori, the group's tribal authority. And the spokesman for that authority, Maui Solomon, said the iwi had declined to present themselves as a culture of victims.

The statement was then further complicated by the revelation that by no means all Moriori agreed with that decision. And one of the iwi's senior kaumatua, Wilford Davis, strongly dissented from it. He felt that a compromise had been made because some Moriori shared Maori ancestry, and because of Moriori fisheries claims, whose success was dependent to some extent on the goodwill of mainland Maori, particularly those who sat on the Waitangi Fisheries Commission.

As an historian with a strong association with the Chathams, my own view was that Te Papa's exhibit was a major advance on the way Moriori culture had been presented in previous museum displays, and I agreed that Moriori themselves had the right to be fully consulted about the content of such displays.

I did not think that the final decision about theme and content should be that of the iwi concerned alone, however, and, as an historian, I thought it odd that more substantial reference was not made to the 1835 invasion — because it was that event that confirmed the nature and ethos of Moriori culture and conditioned decisively what Moriori became in the 20th century.

I did not consider references to Rwanda or the Balkans were especially helpful, but I did think that leaving the Ngati Tama/Ngati Mutunga invasion out of Moriori history was tantamount to trying to explain the situation of the East Timorese without reference to the Indonesian invasion.

Certainly, I would be uncomfortable if Ken Gorbey's comments on behalf of the museum implied that information about aspects of the past ought to be suppressed if they gave comfort to rednecks. That is not a sound reason for misrepresenting history. The only healthy way to deal with the past, and to understand it, is to have all the relevant incidents and episodes out on the table and to be even-handed in the way in which we deal with them.

Cheryl Sotheran was quoted in *The Dominion* as saying that the Moriori exhibit reflected Te Papa's commitment to scholarship and to Matauranga Maori — knowledge founded on Maori custom, culture and protocol.

In the same article, Massey University historian Danny Keenan said that Matauranga Maori gives a voice to Maori who want to contribute to mainstream scholarship and allows them to "frame the issues in a way which reflects Maori ways of doing things".

To the dissenting historians, however, Western scholarship and Matauranga Maori served incompatible ends: Matauranga Maori was a belief system designed to bond people into a community, whereas scholarship and science were "based on the application of unrestricted criticisms and scrutiny of all beliefs . . . to obtain the best possible knowledge of the world".

Miles Fairburn was further quoted as saying that the "relativistic approach" gave too little defence against self-serving depictions of history. "Distinguishing scholarship from this kind of expressing of history is akin to a car owner comparing the report of an expert mechanic with the patter of a salesman."

He added: "If history is to be stated solely or most authentically by descendants, then only Germans can write the history of the Nazis, only Japanese their country's war history."

I would have to say that I agree with the thrust of Fairburn's comment. But, having witnessed many times the intensity of Maori debate over aspects of whanau or iwi history, and the vigorous Maori examination of competing tribal resource claims, I think he underestimates the rigour of the process of internal critiquing involved in Matauranga Maori.

It seems to me, however, that this whole issue of the compatibility or incompatibility of the two systems of knowledge and their respective methodologies ought to be the focus of a major debate between the New Zealand Historical Association and its Maori counterpart, Pouhere Korero. And that the debate ought to occur in a professional forum before it becomes a source of conflict and blood-letting in the mainstream media.

&

Whina Cooper: An Obituary

This feature, first published in The Dominion *in March 1994, was written to commemorate the death of Whina Cooper, whose biography King had written a decade earlier.*

OF COURSE, NOBODY IS INDESTRUCTIBLE. But there were times when I seriously considered the possibility that Whina Cooper might be. So long as she was *determined* to live, it seemed, she would.

Dame Whina survived one serious illness convinced that God had appeared to her ("a short chap with a Pakeha face and a long beard"). He told her that her work was not finished. That was just before the Maori Land March in 1975. In recent years, in her late nineties, she bounced back from a broken hip, a heart attack and a stroke.

People she outmanoeuvred in the course of her extraordinarily long public life, such as the formidable John Rangihau of Tuhoe, said they would settle scores at her tangi. They were all younger than she was. And, with one exception, she outlived them.

My favourite story about her tactical ability concerns a Mill Hill Catholic priest, Father Patrick McCrory. When Dame Whina wanted to bury a nephew, who had committed suicide, in consecrated ground at the Panguru cemetery, Father McCrory said she could not. So Dame Whina buried the nephew outside the cemetery, in a plot where pre-Christian Maori remains had gone. Then she lifted the fence to bring both urupa inside the boundary.

This ability to improvise brilliantly — to come up triumphantly with a course of action that left opponents wrong-footed — was the main expression of Dame Whina's genius. It was also a characteristic that marked her out as a product of her times. The rangatira who had been her mentors in Panguru in her childhood and early adulthood, such as her father Heremia Te Wake, solved problems in this manner (and sometimes created new ones).

Dame Whina was less comfortable in the modern Maori world, where rangatiratanga is seen to reside in group decision making and where projects have to be researched, documented and budgeted. She preferred to trust her instinct and to rely on the inspiration of the moment to say the right thing and carry the day. This approach served her, and those she led, well for most of her life. But it was the source of stress in her time as president of the Maori Women's Welfare League and leader of the Maori Land March.

The most remarkable thing about Dame Whina's life was that it was long and so actively long. She was born into the Te Rarawa tribe on the shores of the Hokianga Harbour in 1895, when Richard Seddon was prime minister and Queen Victoria still had six years left to reign. She led her first protest action — to prevent a Pakeha farmer developing the Panguru mudflats — the year World War One broke out.

She was associated with all the great names of the first Maori revival: Sir James Carroll, who paid her secondary school fees; Sir Peter Buck, who regularly stayed in her home; Sir Apirana Ngata, with whom she instituted land development schemes in Hokianga. Part of Dame Whina's mana and mystique came from the fact that she had walked and talked with these men and been their protégé. Princess Te Puea was a friend and near contemporary.

In her early adulthood, she rapidly became the dominant Maori leader in northern Hokianga. She ran a successful dairy farm and founded a local branch of the Farmers' Union. She established a profitable general store. She built and administered the community centre. She coached the local football team and was elected president of the North Hokianga Rugby Union — and all at a time when women's involvement in the sport was more conventionally confined to washing jerseys and making suppers. She won shooting trophies at the Hokianga Gun Club. And she raised six children from two marriages.

After the death of her second husband in 1949, she moved to Auckland to help her people adjust to the consequences of the Maori urban migration. She fought for better housing for Maori, for more adequate health care for Maori women and children, and she raised funds for Maori cultural activities and facilities in the city.

In 1951 she became a national figure as foundation president of the Maori Women's Welfare League, a position she held for six years. Subsequently she was responsible for the opening in 1966 of Te Unga Waka, New Zealand's first urban marae, and for the Maori Land March from Te Hapua to Parliament in 1975 — the gesture which, more than any other, ignited the Maori cultural and political renaissance of the past two decades. Her protégés from these Auckland years included Dame Mira Szaszy and Dame Kiri Te Kanawa.

She knew and worked with every prime minister from George Forbes through to Jim Bolger (fourteen of them). She objected publicly to the enforced resignation of Sir Apirana Ngata from Cabinet in 1934, and was still around to do the same when Winston Peters was forced to resign nearly sixty years later. Her favourite politician, and the one most like her, was Sir Robert Muldoon.

Honours were heaped on her in her later years: the MBE, CBE, DBE and the Order of New Zealand. But the one that meant most to her was that bestowed by the Maori Women's Welfare League: Te Whaea o te Motu, Mother of the Nation. And, indeed, this was the role in which she basked, and presided over Waitangi commemorations, in her final years.

She reached her largest audience when she welcomed competitors, spectators and television viewers to the opening of the Commonwealth Games in January 1990. And what she said then was a summary of the message she repeated constantly in the last years and months of her life: "Let us all remember that the treaty was signed so that we could all live as one nation in Aotearoa. The challenge before us is . . . to strive for success."

Last week she went home to die under Panguru Mountain, in whose shadow she had been born ninety-eight years ago, and to fulfil a prophecy of her ancestor Tamatea:

> Ka hoki nei ahau ki Panguru, ki Papata,
> Ki te rakau tu Patapata I tu
> Ki te hauauru,

Te angaanga I titi iho I te rangi.
Tu te ra, tu te po.

I shall return to Panguru, to Papata,
To the tree that stands tall
In the west wind,
To the calm that descends from heaven
Day and night.

&

Moriori: A Pride Reborn

Published in New Zealand Geographic, *no. 20, October-December 1993. The essay was an attempt to make clear to a confused audience who Moriori were, and where they came from.*

*W*HEN I FIRST VISITED the Chatham Islands in December 1986, I believed it was to write a requiem for an extinct culture.

The invitation had come from Maui Solomon, grandson of Tommy Solomon, the so-called last Moriori, who had died in 1933. Maui explained that his family had commissioned a statue of Tommy as a memorial to him and to all Moriori people. It was to be unveiled by the Prime Minister at Manukau, the only remaining Moriori reserve on Chatham Island. The family trust established to raise the statue wanted also to commission a book on the history of the Moriori people. Would I write it?

My interest in Moriori history and culture was long-standing. When I was at primary school in the 1950s, I had heard a talk about the Chatham Islands from a man who had worked there as a radio operator. The presentation included colour slides of Moriori carvings on trees and rocks.

Stimulated by that introduction, I subsequently read most of the literature about the Moriori. This revealed a massive confusion in the public mind about who they were and where they had come from. Some of the early New Zealand ethnographers, such as Stephenson Percy Smith and Elsdon Best, had maintained that they were a Melanesian or part-Melanesian race who had occupied New Zealand before the Maori. According to this view, the Moriori had been driven from New Zealand by the more intelligent and assertive Polynesian arrivals, and their remnants had taken refuge in the Chatham Islands.

All such nonsense had been disproved by the professional ethnologist Henry Skinner as early as 1923, when he published his pioneering book, *The Morioris of the Chatham Islands*. From an analysis of material culture, particularly artefacts, Skinner showed beyond doubt that the Moriori were Polynesian, that the special features of their culture had evolved on the Chathams, and that their probable place of origin immediately prior to the Chathams was New Zealand.

For some reason, possibly because the book was published in Honolulu, possibly because the real story was not as appealing as the myths, Skinner's measured and scholarly findings failed to penetrate the public consciousness. Teachers in New Zealand primary schools continued to tell tales about the Moriori being a mysterious and inferior race. Books by amateur ethnologists claimed that they had been dark-skinned, repulsive-looking and shifty. And nearly all New Zealand newspapers at some time carried letters to the editor that asserted that what the Pakeha had done to the Maori by way of colonisation was no more than what the Maori had done to the Moriori. This in turn bred another myth. In denying Maori mistreatment of the Moriori on the mainland, some Maori denied that there ever had been a people called Moriori, either in New Zealand or on the Chatham Islands.

Meantime, New Zealand papers had formally announced the extinction of the Moriori when Tommy Solomon died in March 1933. The Press Association paid tribute to him as "the last pure-blood survivor of the ancient Moriori race". And a journalist who described his burial ended with the words:

"Twilight faded into darkness, and the dull roar of the ocean breakers echoed along the lonely sandhills, as it had echoed before the Moriori came to his new home seven hundred years ago, and as it would continue to echo though he no longer heard its call."

This much I knew in 1986: there had been a people called Moriori, they were Polynesian, they had lived on the Chatham Islands, the largest of which they called Rekohu ('Misty Skies'), their culture had been documented extensively by the farmer-ethnologist Alexander Shand in the latter part of the nineteenth century, and it had, in effect, ceased to be a living culture around 1900 when the last of the Moriori who spoke their language died.

What I did not know was how Moriori descendants viewed their history and their identity more than fifty years after Tommy Solomon's death. I did not know, because on this issue the literature was silent. The only way I could find out was to travel to the Chathams and speak with the people themselves.

The thing that surprised me most about the Chatham Islands on that first visit was the fact that they were so much like the image I had formed of them from reading and listening to travellers' tales. There were the volcanic cones rising from the mist and the sea; there the imprint of the Moriori carved into limestone rock and the trunks of kopi trees; there the abandoned trypots, stone fireplaces and whale bones that could have come from a Herman Melville novel; there the sparse akeake trees twisted and bent by relentless winds over a harsh landscape; and there the people — descendants of sealers, whalers and missionaries who looked every bit as weather-beaten and as durable as the rocks and the surviving trees.

And there, too, were the Moriori. That was the second surprise. They were far from extinct. They were alive and flexing, a forceful presence in Chatham Island affairs. The fact that they were not 'pure blood' turned out to be as irrelevant to the sense of ethnicity as it is to Maori, Pakeha or English folk. They were descended from Moriori. They identified as Moriori. End of equation.

Many, of course, were Solomons. Old Tommy alone has more than one hundred descendants, most of whom now live in mainland New Zealand. But the Solomon presence and the Solomon mana has been kept alive on the Chathams by the sons and grandchildren of Bully Solomon, Tommy's second son. Their resemblance to Tommy is startling and an ample refutation of the notion that a people had died with him.

There were also the Preeces, descendants of an even larger Moriori clan, the Riwais. In 1986, one Preece, Charlie, was introduced to me as the senior Moriori elder on Chatham Island. Another, Bunty, was chairman of the county council. Still another, Riwai, was about to become the island's Anglican vicar. And the next generation of the family was deeply involved, on Chatham and Pitt, in the island's primary occupations of fishing and farming.

There are other Moriori clans, too: the Tamihanas or Thompsons descended from Tamihana Heta, who lived in a huge homestead at Wairau until the 1930s; the Davises, descended from Ani Davis, whose family came back to the Chathams in the 1890s via the Auckland Islands, Foveaux Strait and Port Underwood; the Ashtons, whose bones lie alongside Solomons and Riwais at Manukau; and others whose Moriori links have merged with Maori and Pakeha associations. Most were represented on Chatham Island at the time of the statue unveiling. Almost all were enthusiastic about the notion of a written Moriori history.

Maui Solomon, son of Tommy's eldest son and chairman of the trust which raised the statue, was the most emphatic: a book was needed to dispel the pejorative myths that had grown up around the origin and identity of the Moriori. Bunty Preece agreed, and said he wanted his children and grandchildren to know that they were Moriori, and to learn what it meant. Charlie Preece junior, son of the island's senior elder, said he wanted to ensure that the voices of his Moriori ancestors continued to be heard down the corridors of passing years.

There was only one Moriori who expressed reservations to me. Riwai Preece, who was returning to live in the Chathams after spending most of his adult life in the racing industry in Christchurch, feared that turning a historical focus on Moriori history and experience would have divisive effects on island life. In particular, he feared that it would exacerbate tension between Moriori and Maori, with adverse consequences for the Chatham Islands community as a whole.

He was right. The relationship between Moriori and Maori on the Chathams was one that is potentially uncomfortable. While there is no truth in the notion that Moriori were driven from the New Zealand mainland by Maori, the coming together of the two peoples in the 19th century was even more traumatic for the Moriori than the mythical clash which supposedly exiled Moriori to the islands.

In November and December 1835, the brig *Rodney* carried two shiploads of Ngati Mutunga and Ngati Tama Maori from Port Nicholson to Chatham Island: around nine hundred men, women and children in all (with seventy-eight tonnes of seed potatoes, twenty pigs and seven canoes).

They landed at Whangaroa, took time to recover from the voyage, being nursed and fed by local Moriori, and then began to formally takahi — walk the land — to claim it according to their tikanga or custom. They ritually killed around three hundred Moriori to confirm this claim.

"We were terrified," a survivor, Minarapa, told a government agent three decades later. [We] fled to the bush, concealed ourselves in holes underground, and in any place to escape. . . . It was of no avail. We were discovered and killed — men, women and children. . . ."

The thirteen hundred survivors were enslaved and forbidden to marry, speak their language or practise their culture. "Men were separated from women, parents from children, older children from younger children, and the strings of their heart quivered," Moriori petitioners told Governor George Grey in 1862.

Moriori tikanga forbade fighting, even in self-defence. Consequently, they became a subjugated and demoralised people for the next twenty-seven years.

Ernst Dieffenbach, who visited the Chathams in 1840, noted that they were "the labourers and porters of their masters, who have no notion of anything like moderation in the labour they exact: so that ulcerated backs bent almost double, and emaciated paralytic limbs, with diseased lungs, are the ordinary lot of these ill-fated wretches, to whom death must be a blessing."

Most Moriori took advantage of that "blessing". By the time the slaves were released in 1862, Moriori numbers had plummeted to around one hundred and sixty — one-tenth of the 1835 population. The islands had been annexed to New Zealand in 1842, but it took the passage of two decades before the imposition of New Zealand law was sufficiently effective to give Moriori the same rights and privileges that Maori and Pakeha enjoyed on the mainland.

In 1870, after eight years of agitation by Moriori survivors for redress for the wrongs done to them, the Native Land Court sat in Waitangi to hear competing claims for the islands lodged by Maori and Moriori. Moriori took it for granted that 'British justice' would restore what had been taken from them by force. They contested the Maori assertion of ownership of the islands by conquest on the ground that Moriori, according to the dictates of their tikanga, had not fought; where there was no fighting there could be no conquest.

The Native Land Court Judge, John Rogan, was deaf to Moriori arguments. As he saw it, he was a New Zealand official sitting in a New Zealand court. And the Native Land Court on the mainland based its decisions on tikanga Maori: it applied the so-called 1840 rule, which required judges to give primary weight to circumstances as they were at the time of British annexation of New Zealand — not before.

Judge Rogan found in favour of the Maori claimants. He awarded them ownership of some 97 percent of the islands' territory, reserving a mere 2.7 percent for the subsistence of the unsuccessful Moriori litigants.

This decision was a blow almost as crushing to the morale of Moriori as the 1835 invasion itself had been. They tried in 1885 to win ownership of the offshore birding islands, but these were deemed to have been awarded to Maori in the 1870 decision.

Without the redress they had expected, and without adequate economic resources to support a cultural and demographic recovery, Moriori continued to decline: there were twenty-seven left in 1889, twelve in 1900, six in 1904 and two by 1922. Tommy Solomon was the last.

These figures were, of course, misleading. They referred, as did Maori statistics of the time, to people of so-called 'pure blood'. And while the number of 'pure blood' Moriori was falling rapidly, Moriori of 'mixed blood' were increasing slowly. The Riwais, the Solomons, the Tamihanas and others all had Moriori-Maori descendants and eventually Moriori-Maori-Pakeha descendants. The Davises had Moriori-Negro-Amerindian descendants. Many of these, particularly the Solomons and Preeces, continued to identify as Moriori. Many did not: some because it was more advantageous to be regarded as Maori; others because they were persuaded that Moriori had indeed been an inferior people, and that such ancestry was a source of shame.

These latter simply became Chatham Island Maori. And most Maori on the Chathams came to terms with the events of 1835 and 1870 by regarding Maori and Moriori as one people. In their minds, their separate identities of victor and vanquished had been blended by the passage of time and by intermarriage.

Even those Moriori who treasured and nurtured their separate mana and their tangata whenua status did not flaunt these things in front of their Maori friends, believing that it would be un-Moriori to do so. They spoke of them among themselves, and to interested Pakeha who visited the Chathams, such as Henry Skinner and the conchologist A W Baden Powell. This *modus vivendi*, along with Moriori forbearance, was responsible for the reasonably even tenor of Chatham Islands life. And it persisted until the 1980s, when a group of new factors and circumstances combined to upset it.

One was the Maori cultural renaissance in New Zealand, echoes of which reached the Chathams when islanders returned home. Some claimed that Maori identity had been too much absorbed into a general Chatham Islands culture, and that it was time to reassert mana Maori and to consider making resource claims — particularly concerning the lucrative Chathams fishery — to the Waitangi Tribunal.

At the same time, there was evidence of a reawakening of Moriori identity. In 1980 Television New Zealand had screened a documentary, made by Bill Saunders, on Moriori history. The Solomon family had held a reunion and decided to raise the statue of Tommy at Manukau. Both events led to talk of an eventual revival of Moriori language and culture.

Some Chatham Islanders — Moriori, Maori and Pakeha — were unsettled by what were beginning to look like disruptions to the social and cultural pattern of island life. Riwai Preece was one of them. He told me in 1986 that there had been considerable unity and unanimity among islanders in his lifetime. "We are all one people. And our elders represent all of us, whatever our background. This talk of 'Maori' and 'Moriori' and 'Pakeha' — it divides us up in a way that we're not used to."

It was a cry from the heart and a position of utter sincerity. But it was only one voice. Others saw a written history as an essential cultural resource to support the burgeoning Moriori renaissance and to decisively clear away the destructive myths of the past. Still others were offended and hurt by the growing inclination of a small number of Maori on Chatham Island to speak of themselves as tangata whenua without reference to the tuakana status of Moriori (who had, after all, occupied the islands for at least five hundred years longer than Maori).

For these people, an acknowledgment of what had transpired in the past was a prerequisite for future Moriori-Maori co-operation. They were especially wounded by the insistence of one kaumatua of Ngati Mutunga that, in spite of the traditional and historical evidence, and in spite of the testimony of Maori before the Native Land Court in 1870, there had been no Moriori killed as a consequence of the 1835 invasion.

For a mainlander, many features of this cultural and historical equation were unusual. The sequence of settlement in New Zealand had been Maori, then European, and Europeans had colonised the Maori; on the Chathams the sequence had been Moriori, European, a
and Maori had colonised the Moriori.

Just as Maori could be said to hold the moral high ground on the mainland, Moriori — because of their status as victims — occupied that position on the Chathams. And just as Maori rightly claimed in New Zealand that they were being denied full acknowledgment of their tangata whenua status and the rights that flowed from that, so on the Chathams it was Moriori who made this claim. They had lost the vast bulk of their land, their fishing rights, their birding rights, and a large part of their physical and material culture. By the mid-1980s they were even having difficulty retaining their speaking rights on the Chatham Island marae. The Maori, who were by this time planning to lodge a Waitangi Tribunal claim for the Chathams fishery, intended to do so without any reference to Moriori rights.

It was these factors and others which convinced me that, despite the possibility of social disharmony, the Moriori history had to be written.

I worked on the project over the next three years. Some of the information that needed to be gathered into the narrative lay in the Chathams, in the collective memories of Moriori families. Although people kept telling me how much of the Moriori history and culture had been lost, I was continually surprised by how much individuals remembered of things that parents and grandparents had told them: the correct practices for catching fish and gathering shellfish; the rules of tapu that applied when water was being used for different purposes; the use of Chathams gentian as a contraceptive; and other things of this sort.

The most vivid recollections were those of Moriori individuals: Tommy Solomon, genial and generous; Tommy's father Rangitapua, a dignified and solemn man; Riwai Te Ropiha, who doused one of his jockeys with women's scent on Chatham Islands race day, because the boy hadn't washed recently; Arthur Lockett, who assumed leadership of the Moriori iwi when Tommy Solomon died; and Bill Davis, who was remembered as being a shrewd businessman and an articulate spokesman for Chathams interests.

Some of the most moving stories, however, came from former islanders living in New Zealand. Jane Hough, a nonagenarian in Taupo, told me how her aunt had got to her feet to karanga Tommy the last time he appeared at the race course near Waitangi in December 1931:

"She called out in Maori to Tommy, to his father and mother, and to all those other Moriori old people she had known who were now dead. And she called out to the tipua Moriori — the spirits that the Moriori had been able to raise in the days when they ruled the island. . . . It was her way of saluting him and farewelling him, and of acknowledging that his people were the first people on the island. Tommy didn't say anything. He just stopped the sledge and listened to her, with his head bowed. The tears were rolling down his cheeks."

The fullest accounts of Moriori experience, and the richest, turned out to be preserved in documents. There were the writings of Alex Shand, who had ridden around Chatham Island with Hirawanu Tapu between 1868 and 1900, speaking with all Moriori whose recollections went beyond the period of Maori occupation. This corpus preserved most of what we know today about Moriori language and culture.

Of even greater significance, however, were the writings of Moriori themselves. In the papers of Sir George Grey, held in the Auckland Public Library, lay two major Moriori manuscripts. One, written in 1859 by elders of the Otonga tribe, is made up of historical and genealogical information which emphasises the difference between Moriori and Maori (although, ironically, it is largely written in Maori, the language of the colonisers).

The other, one hundred and thirty-one pages in Moriori and Maori, is the proceedings of a council of Moriori elders held at Te Awapatiki in 1862. It records their recollection of the Maori invasion twenty-seven years earlier, ("November must have been the month, for we were drinking honey from the flax-flowers when they landed"), and it lists all adult Moriori alive in 1835, and details what became of them ("know by looking at this that those with two crosses by their names were killed and eaten"). It closes with a plea to Grey to restore Moriori land to its former owners.

In addition to these documents, a large number of Moriori letters survived from the 19th century. Some had been collected on Chatham Island in the 1930s and 1940s by a Post Office radio technician, Bill Burt, and eventually deposited in the Turnbull Library. Others survived in the papers of Tom Ritchie, a Northern Irishman who had come to the Chathams in 1864 and farmed there for nearly sixty years. He employed Moriori farmhands and stockmen, many of whom wrote letters to him about their crises and rites of passage: "Rau has died . . . I have seen the accounts for Rau's long-timer [long-term debt] and the accounts for the sheep. I will find payment for the long-timers after his funeral. I send you my love. I am greatly distressed . . ."

The most important set of surviving Moriori papers, however, came to light after the book was published.

I had devoted considerable time, unsuccessfully, trying to find out what had become of Bill Davis. Davis, Moriori on his mother's side, had grown up in the 1890s and early 1900s at Hawaruwaru. As the last of the Moriori elders sickened and died, they bequeathed their papers to him, believing that he would carry what was left of Moriori culture into the modern world.

They were right about identifying Davis as a man of ability and integrity. He enlisted as a private in World War One and came home a second lieutenant. By 1940, he was a successful farmer and chairman of the county council. Then he left the islands and nobody there had heard from him since.

In January 1990, I took a phone call from a man who told me that I wouldn't know him, but that his name was Wilford Davis. I said at once: "Bill Davis's son!" And so he was. And he told me that he had "a few papers that might interest you".

Bill Davis had died at Laingholm in Auckland in 1962, and his son Wilf had found a box of fragile documents written in pencil and ink. He had looked at them, seen that they appeared to be in Maori, and stored them away. Early in 1990, as a consequence of reading *Moriori, A People Rediscovered*, he got them out again, and contacted me.

It was a moving experience for both of us to sort through the papers. Here were whakapapa, waiata, stories, information on Moriori tribal boundaries, navigation instructions, letters to people in government, and much more. All had been painstakingly written by elderly men in smoky ponga huts in the latter part of the 19th century. Some pages still smelt of peat smoke and tobacco. Miraculously, they had survived. Collectively, they amounted to a treasure trove of cultural and historical information, significant and enduring messages that Moriori ancestors had sent to their descendants.

I would, of course, have been grateful for knowledge of the Davis papers before the book was written. But, as it turned out, there was nothing in them that contradicted the evidence of other sources. They extended and elaborated the Moriori story rather than recast it.

And that story, in brief, is that the ancestors of the Moriori almost certainly came to the Chathams from mainland New Zealand. They carried with them the East Polynesian styles of ornament- and tool-making that they shared with early Maori. They also carried New Zealand materials with which to make these tools, especially argillite and obsidian, and a range of names for trees, birds and fish.

Over the centuries that followed, this founding population expanded and developed a culture that in some important respects differed from that of their cousins in mainland New Zealand. Chatham Island Polynesians outlawed warfare, largely discarded notions of rank, abandoned horticulture and developed their own dialect. This was the culture that came to be known in the nineteenth century as Moriori.

Their artefacts and technology seemed to observers to be more primitive than that of other Polynesians. Their waka korari or reed canoes, for example, were slow and cumbersome craft, difficult to steer and half inundated with water. Yet, by using water as a natural ballast, they were perfectly adapted to Chatham Islands conditions. They remained stable in the rough seas around the islands. Maori laughed at them in 1835. But the dugout canoes which Ngati Mutunga and Ngati Tama brought with them turned turtle off the Chathams, and tipped their crews into the sea. From then on, until the arrival of European boats, the birding and the fishing was done for Maori by Moriori in waka korari.

Moriori people and Moriori identity survived the traumas of the seal slaughter of the early 19th century, the introduction of European diseases, the Maori invasion and the unfavourable decisions of the Native Land Court.

In the period that I was writing the book, Moriori lodged a claim with the Waitangi Tribunal for compensation for their loss of physical and cultural resources as a consequence of Maori and Pakeha colonisation of the Chathams.

By the 1990s, they had joined the National Maori Congress as tangata whenua of the Chathams, and they were negotiating successfully for quota from the Maori Fisheries Commission. They were again using Moriori language and waiata for their rituals of welcome (on the occasion of the bicentenary of Lieutenant Broughton's rediscovery of Chatham Island in 1791, for example).

Moriori people not only have an accessible and well documented past, they now have an assured future. And plans for that future include the building of a marae on Chatham Island, the holding of whare wananga to educate their iwi in Moriori language and culture, and the establishment of tourism and fishing ventures to generate employment for Moriori on the Chathams and income for further cultural development.

Charlie Preece junior, now chairman of Te Iwi Moriori Trust Board, estimates the number of identifiable Moriori descendants to be between three hundred and one thousand. He has boundless optimism about the opportunities now opening up for his people.

"We have not only survived in the face of impossible odds over the past two hundred years, we have flourished in spite of them. We stand proud with our whanaunga from Aotearoa as we develop our fisheries and rejuvenate our cultural roots. We do these things not as an appendage of any mainland tribe, not as vassals of our so-called conquerors. We assert our own mana and our own tino rangatiratanga as Moriori, the first people of Rekohu."

&

The Chathams Debate

Published in Mana *magazine, April/May 1993, when the debate between Maori and Moriori as to who were tangata whenua of the Chatham Islands was at its height. It also reflects a fear on the part of historians that they were being used as 'hired guns' in the Maori resource claims process.*

*T*HE BRITISH *BOOKSELLER* MAGAZINE recently described the public's perception of a Queen's Counsel. "Quick master of a brief (anyone's brief), get a good case together, put a good face on it (more like a mask, really), then out with the silver tongue to persuade the jury that it's your chap who's right."

This has a counterpart in New Zealand in a similar view of the modern historian: someone who will likewise master a brief, select the evidence that supports it, then argue eloquently in favour of the cause that is paying the fee. The fact that aspects of New Zealand history have recently become exceedingly contentious, that they have consequences for resource allocations, and that historians have become involved in competing claims before the Waitangi Tribunal — all this only strengthens the perception of them as hired guns.

The parallel is unfortunate and wrong. There is a difference in kind between the approach of the lawyer and the methodology of the historian. Lawyers are indeed given a brief and have a responsibility to argue it as persuasively as possible whether or not they believe in the validity or justice of the case. Professional historians, on the other hand, are expected to investigate a question open-mindedly, gather the evidence, weigh it in a disinterested manner, then draw fair conclusions that arise solely out of that evidence.

That doesn't mean that historians don't have opinions, sometimes strong and controversial opinions. They do. It just means that they have reached them by a very different process from that employed by members of the legal profession.

The other thing professional historians are not inclined to do, which pressure groups do as a matter of course, is argue polemically. Pressure groups have an axe to grind, often a perfectly legitimate axe, and they take every opportunity to bring their case before the public, dramatise it, overstate it, score points over their opponents, and generally use the evidence available in any way which promotes the outcome they seek.

It is not the role of the historian to be involved in this process, other than by saying: "Here is the evidence. This is what we know and don't know. Draw your own conclusions."

Nowhere are these issues more alive and contentious than in the Chatham Islands. The Chathams have a somewhat different history, and a different ethnic equation, from those that apply on the New Zealand mainland. The first people to settle the islands, six hundred or more years ago, were Polynesian immigrants who came to be known as Moriori: the second group were Europeans, who rediscovered the islands in 1791, exploited them for the next three decades and settled there from 1827; and the third group were Maori, who invaded the islands in 1835 and subsequently claimed sovereignty by right of conquest.

Even that simple sequence gives little idea of the additional complexities of the situation. Maori, according to their values, did conquer the Moriori. They walked the land, ritually killed around three hundred Chatham Islanders and enslaved the remainder. They followed their tikanga for that set of circumstances.

Moriori, on the other hand, had a different tikanga. They had outlawed fighting. For them, retention of their mana, including their mana whenua, was dependent on not taking up arms. They argued, therefore, that they were never defeated and never relinquished their mana whenua.

Most Chatham Islanders — Moriori, Maori and Pakeha — are well aware of this situation and are philosophical about it and tolerant of one another's presence. Individuals alive at the present time can hardly be held responsible for the actions of their ancestors. Besides, many islanders are descended from all three ethnic groups.

Matters became more contentious in the 1980s, however, when two sets of events coincided and interrupted the relatively even tenor of island life. The revival of Maori culture and identity on the mainland was matched by a revival of Moriori and Maori identity on the Chathams; and the prospect of tangata whenua claims for major economic resources, particularly the Chathams fishery, resulted in the formation of competing iwi groups to pursue those claims.

Maori claimants before the Waitangi Tribunal for the Chathams fishery include the Taranaki Maori Trust Board (because the 1835 invaders, Ngati Mutunga and Ngati Tama, came originally from Taranaki), and Te Runanga O Wharekauri Rekohu, representing Maori currently living in the Chathams. Moriori claimants include the Tchakat Henu Association, representing some of the Moriori on Chatham Island, including members of the Solomon family, and Te Iwi Moriori, representing other Moriori on the island and most of those now living on the mainland.

With these broad battlelines drawn, they condition a myriad smaller issues which arise on the Chathams almost month by month. And almost all of those issues involve the use or misuse of history.

The Chatham Islands Conservation Board, for example, has been having drawn-out discussions on whether or not to have either or both of the main island's indigenous names on its letterhead. Some Maori representations favour the use of Wharekauri, the name Maori gave to Chatham Island in the 1830s.

The Moriori representations, made in person and in writing by the two iwi groups, argued for Rekohu, the original and Moriori name for the island. Most board members felt that both ancestral names should be used, reflecting both heritages, and they proposed to render them Rekohu/Wharekauri, the order in which they had occurred.

This satisfied none of the iwi organisations. The Moriori groups argued that Rekohu and Rekohu alone was the tangata whenua name; the runanga responded by arguing that Rekohu was a name that had only been in use "for the past six or seven years" and that Wharekauri dated from "circa 11th century" and should therefore take precedence over Rekohu. A written submission from the rununga went on to argue:

"'Rekohu/Wharekauri' grossly contradicts traditional history passed down by our tupuna . . . In respect of Wharekauri, much history was written by early missionary settlers and whalers, disgruntled settlers who could not secure freehold entitlements to land, who came with a manuhiri perspective. They did not have a full appreciation of the oral language spoken nor did they fully understand or know the traditional or historical journeys of the people (the early people or Maruiwi) to these islands."

Disturbed by these claims, the Conservation Board asked the chairman of the runanga to lay on the table his sources of information for the claim that the name Wharekauri dates "from the 11th century". He declined to do so. He said the board would have to do its own research. The board did so.

What it found was that, far from dating from "the past six or seven years", the name Rekohu occurred in the earliest manuscript material written in the Chatham Islands in the 1850s and 1860s. Moriori oral tradition was that Rekohu, meaning "misty skies", had always been their tupuna name for the main island.

Wharekauri, according to the 19th century Maori informants Hohepa Tamaihengia, Teonga Te Poke, Rakatau Katihe and others, was the Maori name given in the 1830s to a small settlement on the north coast of the Chatham Island which the invading Ngati Mutunga and Ngati Tama gave to the whole island, because they found it easier to pronounce than the Moriori Rekohu.

So what was the evidence "from traditional sources" that the runanga had refused to identify? Its origin was given away by the use of the term "Maruiwi" and mention of "the 11th century". Alas, it was not Maori traditional evidence at all. It came from Stephenson Percy Smith's book, *The Lore of the Whare-Wananga*. This purported to be the teachings of a learned Maori tohunga called Matorohanga, which had been written down by Whatahoro Jury. Those "teachings", as anyone with a grounding in Maori history is aware, are now known to be forgeries.

The first person to dismiss them as spurious was the great Ngati Mutunga scholar, Sir Peter Buck, (whose Maori name, Te Rangi Hiroa, came from his maternal uncle who drowned in Te Whanga lagoon on Chatham Island shortly before Buck was born). He wrote in *The Coming of the Maori* (1950) that the Matorohanga/Whatahoro Jury version of the discovery of the Chathams was "an extraordinary compilation of so many details [including dates given in anno domini years] that nothing is left for doubt except its authenticity". He accused Whatahoro Jury of "a deliberate plan of conjuring up extra details".

Later, a full analysis of the manuscripts on which *The Lore of the Whare-Wananga* was based was carried out by David Simmons. He found that the first version had been written down in English in 1840 by an Englishman, J M Jury (Whatahoro's father). This was copied into another book, still in English, by another person and given to Whatahoro Jury, who added many embellishments of his own. Percy Smith then copied out Whatahoro's version and translated it back into English. Simmons noted that each translator and copier had added details to the original story derived from what they knew — or thought they knew — about New Zealand history in the late 19th century.

Thus the complete set of teachings and the two books Percy Smith based on them are fraudulent Maori tradition.

This whole episode brought the role of history in current affairs sharply into focus. It is all too easy for anyone who does not know the background and has not canvassed all the relevant evidence to pick up a copy of *The Lore of the Whare-Wananga* and say: "Hey! Here we have it. Authentic Maori tradition." It is up to the historian to say, "Well, not quite," to lay out fully the evidence on how such a book was compiled, and to compare its conclusions with the earliest authenticated Maori and Moriori traditions which have survived.

This does not represent an historian taking sides on a partisan issue. It is simply part of the process of bringing evidence and context to light in the interests of moving as close to the truth as it is possible to get. What use is made of that evidence will be determined by the warring pressure groups and those who adjudicate on their arguments.

In the case under discussion, Te Runanga O Wharekauri Rekohu changed its tactics once its evidence and argument was discredited. Its most recent communication to the Chatham Islands Conservation Board asked that neither tupuna name appear on the board letterhead.

". . . the island community has never experienced such disharmony and community upheaval through outside influences trying to impose what they think will be 'appropriate' ways that we islanders should live and be . . . The political intervention by outside people has caused us to attack one another in ways that would cause our tupuna to turn over in their graves."

While all this was going on, that same rununga presented a submission to the Waitangi Tribunal arguing that "Moriori no longer exist . . . Moriori as a people have ceased to be." This contention was contested

vigorously by Moriori counter-argument, and the tribunal formally —
and for the first time — recognised Moriori as an iwi and confirmed
their standing in terms of the Treaty of Waitangi legislation.

If nothing else, this sequence of events confirmed something that
historians have always believed, but which politicians and students
sometimes have difficulty accepting: that the past continues to impinge
on the present, that history creates current affairs, that a knowledge of
history is useful; in a phrase, that history is very much alive.

&

The Musket Wars

This is an introduction to the book of the same name by R D Crosby, published by Reed in 1999.

*N*EW ZEALAND HISTORY, in the sense of a written analysis of the country's past based on documentary and oral evidence, has made enormous progress in the past two decades. A greater *quantity* of historical literature has appeared than at any other time, and being largely the work of professionals applying scholarly standards, the *quality* has improved considerably on what had gone before.

Hence we have had two editions of the ground-breaking *The Oxford History of New Zealand*, a series of fine political biographies of 19th and 20th century politicians, and a cluster of books which, for the first time, make adequate use of Maori as well as non-Maori sources to explore our history of race relations and cultural encounter.

The reasons for this florescence are inter-related. One is a growth of cultural nationalism, which has had the effect of making New Zealand readers and writers more interested in the history of their own country than they were a generation ago. Another is the Maori renaissance, which grew both out of a burgeoning literature on Maori experience and also extended the appetite for such books. A third is a turning away of professional historians from themes of global and British imperial history in favour of topics of greater national significance, and a fourth is the activism of New Zealand publishers in seeking to tell specifically New Zealand stories. Finally, the activities of the Waitangi Tribunal have generated a new corpus of information about post-1840 history and a need to disseminate and explain tribunal decisions on major resource claims, such as those of Ngai Tahu in the South Island.

James Belich's seminal book on the New Zealand Wars of the 1840s and 1860s, first published in 1986, and his series of television documentaries based on the book, are among the high points of the florescence I have described. They not only addressed a topic of inherent interest for Maori and Pakeha; they also reached and promulgated conclusions that came as a surprise to many Pakeha New Zealanders — such as the notion that, in every sense that mattered, far from suffering defeat, Maori *won* the war in the North.

The very success of the Belich book and television programmes serve to highlight a criticism made by the author of this volume, however: with the exception of Anne Salmond's two books on the nature and consequences of early Maori-Pakeha contact, and Claudia Orange's research on circumstances leading to the signing of the Treaty of Waitangi, almost none of the flurry of recent historical research and publication has addressed the pre-1840 history of New Zealand.

I see no reason to believe that this lacuna has sinister implications. Two obvious explanations are that the existence of post-1840 documentation makes that period considerably easier logistically to research; and, because of the signing of the Treaty of Waitangi in 1840 and the subsequent application by the Native Land Court and the Maori Land Court of the '1840 rule' (meaning that the baseline for all Maori resource claims through the court and subsequently through the Waitangi Tribunal must be the circumstances that applied in 1840), the major focus of recent Maori-initiated research has also been the post-1840 period.

Ron Crosby is also right to lament this situation. There is a strong argument to be made for the contention that the European presence in New Zealand had long-lasting and (in some respects) devastating effects on Maori life long before the signing of the Treaty of Waitangi. Along with effects of disease on a population without immunity, the most powerful agent of the early transformation of Maori society was the capacity to kill at a distance, which came with the arrival of muskets in the early years of the 19th century.

Before considering the impact of muskets on Maori life, however, it is helpful to consider what the nature of that tribal society was: specifically, what was the cultural context into which muskets and other products of European technology were introduced?

At the time of the rediscovery of New Zealand by Europeans in the 18th century, Maori lived in hapu-based communities in which almost all members, with the exception of slaves, were related by blood or by marriage. The strongest ethic regulating behaviour was the concept of utu or reciprocity, recognised and observed by Maori from North Cape to Stewart Island. This concept meant that relations among individuals and between tribes were governed by an implicit keeping of social accounts: a favour bestowed by a donor required an eventual favour in return from the recipient; and an insult by one, real or imagined, also activated an obligation to reciprocate.

In many respects, and in many places, this cultural equation ensured social stability, particularly within hapu: favours given led to favours returned; koha offered, to koha received; gifts of resources in which one group was rich to an acceptance of other resources within the gift of one's neighbours. In this latter context, utu laid the basis for trading relationships. Where the formula embraced negativities, however — the unauthorised use of resources without the permission of those who had guardianship of them, the passing of an insult, the rape of a female relation — then the response might be a martial one, particularly if the offender was a member of another hapu or tribe.

Because it was intimately connected with the qualities of individual and group mana, this process of social accounting engaged much of the attention of pre-contact Maori society. When the balance of generosity or power was in your favour, your own mana, and that of your people, was enlarged; when you were in debit to your neighbours, your mana was diminished. Living was a matter of continually evening the balance or righting it in one's favour. Sometimes this required you to go to war with your neighbours, or with some distant adversary; if you were successful in combat, this rectified what you had regarded as an imbalance. It may also have rectified matters in the eyes of your neighbour, if your neighbour shared your view of the circumstances which led to the conflict. If your neighbour did not share that view, then the outcome of the most recent engagement became yet another wrong to be righted at some time in the future.

When Maori possessed only hand-to-hand weapons and lacked large quantities of easily portable food, warfare was scarcely ever endemic, usually took place in the summer months only, and most often resulted in the deaths of no more than a handful of combatants (there were exceptions, such as the prolonged campaign of the Marutuahu federation of tribes for mana whenua over the earlier peoples of the Coromandel Peninsula). Nor were all Maori at war with other Maori over a long period of time. When James Cook encountered New Zealanders for the first time in 1769 and 1770, he observed that some of them (at Anaura Bay on the East Coast of the North Island, for example) lived in 'profound peace', without fortifications of any kind; at some other places, such as in the eastern Bay of Plenty, the population clustered in fortified pa in a state of constant readiness for war.

When European muskets became available to northern Maori as a consequence of trading timber and flax in the late 18th and 19th centuries, the first use of them seems to have been in hunting birds. It was not long, however, perhaps no more than a decade, before some Maori appreciated the potential value of such weapons in combat; and the opportunity they presented for settling old scores with a degree of decisiveness never before possible or dreamed of. It was Hongi Hika of Ngapuhi in particular who equipped an army with muskets for battle and potatoes for supplies, and who, in a succession of expeditions, laid waste his tribal opponents on a scale that was unprecedented. In adopting this strategy, Hongi was doing something that Maori in general accomplished with flair: making use of European technology to strengthen Maori values, practices and institutions. His compatriots were to show a similar enthusiasm for European tools, cultivated fruits and vegetables, clothing, even — at a later period — the process of photography. By accepting these features of European material culture and turning them to their own ends, Maori displayed a capacity for adaptability and survival that was virtually unequalled by colonised people elsewhere in the world.

In the case of muskets, however, the disproportionately lethal effect on opponents who lacked them upset the balances of pre-European tribal life and took a terrible toll. In contrast to the pre-contact days, when casualties might be measured in dozens and there were always survivors among the vanquished, now those same casualties might number hundreds or, in a few dramatic instances, thousands. The logistical results of this imbalance of firepower and terror make up the bulk of the narrative of Crosby's book. These results included population movement and displacement on a scale never before seen or envisaged in Maori life: especially the effects of the southward movement of Ngati Toa, Ngati Raukawa and several Taranaki tribes, which had devastating consequences for the people of the Cook Strait region, the South Island, and the Chatham Islands.

Even after the nearly three decades of Maori tribal musket warfare had come to an end — because of Pax Britannica and an eventual balance of firepower achieved when almost all surviving Maori had access to these weapons — the consequences persisted. Some tribes were so weakened as to have virtually lost their identities as separate hapu or iwi; others, largely victors, survived in territories that had not traditionally been their own, and from which they had uprooted tangata whenua of longer standing less than twenty years before the signing of the Treaty of Waitangi. To apply the '1840 rule' to this distribution of people and power has as much logic, and as much fairness, as the application of a hypothetical '1940 rule' would have had on the borders of Europe. And this dislocation occurred, it should be remembered, as a consequence not of the internal dynamics of pre-contact Maori society but of the introduction of European weapons.

The effects of the Musket Wars are felt in New Zealand today: in the current locations of the Maori tribal populations and interpretations of which peoples hold mana whenua over which territories; and in the resentments that some tribes still feel about being displaced from long-held traditional homelands so soon before the Treaty of Waitangi froze an artificially induced distribution of authority for all time. Already one iwi has attempted to use the Waitangi Tribunal structure to challenge this outcome; it seems likely that others will follow. New Zealand has by no means heard the last of the Musket Wars as a source of argument about the distribution of mana whenua.

The Musket Wars will not constitute the last word on this complex topic; but it is a very substantial first word. It will draw deserved and belated attention to the subject, engage the consideration of a professional and non-professional readership, and launch a debate on its significance.

The author, Ron Crosby, is a lawyer. He has not approached his topic in quite the same way as a professional historian might; nor has he been able to canvass all the potential Maori oral sources of information on the multiple tribal encounters that make up the Musket Wars. What he has done, however, by bringing together so much of the written information about these wars into a single volume, is of enormous service to New Zealand history and its consumers. This body of material can now be read in all its breadth; patterns of meaning and significance not apparent in accounts of individual conflicts can be seen against the canvas of the period as a whole; and, as a consequence, the process of analysing and understanding this neglected part of our history can be carried on in earnest.

The best definition of history I know is that of Pieter Geyl, who called the genre 'an argument without end'. To have 'an argument without end', however, it is necessary to have a beginning; in the case of the New Zealand Musket Wars, this book is just such a beginning.

&

Maori Oral History:
Some Cultural and Methodological Considerations

This essay was originally published in the Journal of New Zealand History, *Vol 12, No. 2, October 1978. It followed publication in the previous year of* Te Puea: A Biography.

*L*ATE IN 1974 I BEGAN RESEARCH for a biography of Te Puea Herangi and a related thesis on her life and work. I set out with a clear idea of what I wanted to do and how I intended to go about it. These views had to be modified considerably in the light of conditions encountered in field-work and in the processing of research material. Because I had worked largely without precedents or appropriate models, I felt subsequently that there would be merit in discussing these conditions and difficulties, and the steps I took to meet them.

I planned my research for the parallel studies as a single oral history project. I wanted to represent, as directly as possible, the views of my major informants — most of whom were 'non-literate' in the sense that they preferred oral to written communication (some, in addition, were illiterate). I expected and wanted my research and the subsequent record to reflect the informants' sense of priority and relevance; to emphasise values and incidents that they considered significant, and to de-emphasise those they found less important.

Where the resulting interpretations differed from what I considered to be 'received' or 'European' view, I intended to note and discuss such divergences in footnotes and appendices. The studies were planned, in short, to represent a Waikato Maori view of Te Puea and her times. Documents were to be used largely as aids to memory or to point up shifts of opinion and divergences with previous interpretations.

I had a number of reasons for wanting to conduct the project in this manner. One was the fact that Maori viewpoints had not been well represented in general histories because these had tended to be document-oriented. Discussions of history and public affairs that I heard on Waikato marae over six years were of a markedly different character — in idiom and interpretation — from those that took place in non-Maori circles and in documents. They suggested that there were Maori views of the past with a coherence and validity of their own that deserved to be recorded and considered in the process of national stock-taking called general or social history. The only way to ensure such consideration, it seemed to me, was to try to make oral traditions literary ones.

Second, I suspected that purely document-oriented history ran the risk of being culturally biased to the extent of representing the past unfairly — what Maharaia Winiata called 'Pakeha-coloured' history. One example I heard discussed frequently — and the one to which Winiata was referring specifically — was that of the so-called King Country Pact between the Maniapoto chiefs and John Boyce as Minister of Native Affairs in 1883. Waikato-Maniapoto oral tradition was emphatic that a condition for the opening of the Main Trunk Railway was that alcohol be not allowed in the area. Dr A H McLintock, Parliamentary historian, concluded in 1953 that no such pact was ever made because he could find no evidence for it in Parliamentary records. The Maori explanation was that those responsible for transcribing the relevant meetings did not recognise the Maori case as a significant element in the agreement; whereas for the Maori participants, the no-liquor provision had been a prerequisite.

This kind of discrepancy seemed inevitable when the tradition of one culture was that history lay in records while the other continued to transmit important information orally. In addition, it was probable that on many occasions the transcribers of discussions between Maori and European representatives did not always understand the Maori language, let alone identify the Maori viewpoint. A recording and transcription of oral traditions, therefore, seemed to suggest a way of correcting an inherent imbalance in the historical record.

Third, I was trying to evolve an appropriate model for consideration of Maori-Pakeha social history. Western literary conventions displayed shortcomings when applied to Maori areas of experience. But so did those that were Polynesian in character. An oral record that remained oral was subject to the inevitably warping effects of both the passage of time (failing memories, alterations in transmission and a desire of informants to be seen by posterity in a favourable light) and the cultural function of much oral transmission. I have noted elsewhere that "It is the homily kind of story — the anecdotes that preserve maxims and morals— that flourish most readily in an oral climate, nurtured by frequent oratory and pointed story telling that seek to reinforce . . . myths and values."

One person who had experimented in search of such a model was Pei Te Hurinui in *King Potatau* and (for events to which he was a witness) *Mahinarangi (The Moonglow of the Heavens)*. These books, particularly the first, had obvious strengths. They sought to define for posterity what was significant according to Maori concepts of relevance; and they employed a frequently rhetorical and metaphor-laden Maori idiom. *King Potatau* sought to blend Maori traditions about events and statements of the past according to the author's informed view of which sources were reliable and which courses of action probable.

But both books, on balance, were less than satisfying as models for subsequent literature. Sources were rarely identified so that it was impossible to test reliability or to weigh merits in the case of disagreement. In marae debate, narratives, details and sources could be challenged and elaborated orally; in book form, compiled by a single narrator, they could not. Secondly, the mock-heroic and romantic features of the prose were often highly distasteful in English: "There will be many a tale told of high endeavour, of romance, and of human joy and sorrow. Indeed, many nights will pass unheeded in their telling." "And then stood forth the company of poi dancers . . . Ah me! They were alluringly beautiful. The heart-beat of the scribe still quickens when he describes the lilt, the poise and the seductive allure of those maidens as they sang and danced to a melodious and tuneful ditty."

Pei Te Hurinui did not succeed in conveying the idiom of one language in a form appropriate to the other. He was contrivedly 'literary' in his approach, and his feel for English was not such as to be able to sustain the experiments. Regrettably, the failure was so obtrusive that it tended to blind European readers to other merits in the two books. More recently the writing of Witi Ihimaera and Patricia Grace has shown that in fiction at least it is possible to make the transition of thought and feeling that Te Hurinui attempted in historical writing.

The form that seemed to me most appropriate to meet some of the difficulties was one that would involve writing according to the conventions of Western history and biography (expository prose, clearly labelled sources, footnotes, and some discussion of methodology) but from sources that were Maori — the transcripts of interviews taped with authoritative oral informants. If there were disagreement over facts or interpretations — from Maori or Pakeha quarters — then sources could be identified, returned to, examined and disputed. This seemed an appropriate and reliable way of combining the conventions and the requirements of oral and literary methods.

A fourth consideration was that I wanted the result of my research to be available to my informants. An important justification for what I was doing was that I was recording for Waikato Maori posterity, and that this would have beneficial educational and cultural consequences. Hence I was not only *prepared* to let my sources see the results of my research, I *wanted* them to do so — it was a means of verifying in their eyes and in their terms that what I was doing was socially worthwhile; it would justify effort and time they had devoted to me, and the (to them) eccentric nature of the demands I had made; and for me it was a means of giving back to a community something of what had been taken from its members.

So much for the ideal. I found quickly that it had to be modified constantly; that factors arose which, as far as I knew, had not been professionally or comprehensively discussed previously in New Zealand; and that in seeking to cope with these factors I was to a large extent breaking new ground. Some of the difficulties could be termed methodological — and these could arise in the course of any subsequent New Zealand oral history project. Others could be called cultural and arose out of trying to apply Western research techniques and analytical tools to a Polynesian situation; these would be likely to recur when later researchers applied themselves to Maori topics. Still other problems arose as a combination of methodological *and* cultural factors.

One of the first difficulties was that of establishing, from oral evidence alone, something as fundamental as what apparently happened: sequence, chronology, an acceptable degree of plausibility and accuracy. Memories deteriorated, informants died, and second-hand oral accounts differed (sometimes even first-hand oral accounts differed). Only contemporary documents could give an authoritative account of the composition and sequence of some events, especially those for which there were no longer surviving witnesses.

Second, both sets of resources — oral and documentary — were too thin for either to be relied upon exclusively; nor was either entirely reliable on its own, for reasons I shall discuss. Third, contrary to my expectations, there were documents that either expressed adequately or hinted at the kinds of Maori viewpoints that I had hoped to elicit from oral informants. And fourth, it became apparent that if I pursued the ideal of continuous referral of the results of my research to informants as I had promised, I would be severely inhibited in discussing problems of methodology. Such discussion would appear to informants at best as expressions of doubt or disappointment, and at worst as wounding personal criticism for unreliability or deception.

A further difficulty I had not foreseen was that researchers — if they are to open and retain channels of communication — can find themselves involved unavoidably in the cosmology of their subjects and their rituals. They can find themselves embraced by and drawn inside concepts and values they are hoping only to witness and record. They also find themselves in a position where — if they discuss some of these things — they may be regarded as having broken confidence.

I have noted that "oral research cannot be done precipitately or coldly. It can arise only out of a relationship of ease and trust." This does not mean simply taking time to get to know people, sitting with them, talking with and about their families, taking them to the shops and the doctor, witnessing family feuds and sharing family joys and bereavements. It does mean these things; but it can also mean having to wait while an informant prays before he begins a taping session, having one's tape recorder sprinkled with water to whaka noa or decontaminate it, having to kneel while an informant places his hands on one's head to deliver a Pai Marire blessing, even (in one instance) being invited to enter a river to be blessed and cleansed. All these things occurred in the course of the *Te Puea* project. I would feel I was breaking confidence in the most reprehensible way were I to make these intimacies part of my study; yet I am aware that to ignore them is also to fail in some measure to carry out professional responsibilities.

The major ways in which the shape of the project changed in the course of research were that I became aware of the need to draw simultaneously from documentary and oral sources; that I was going to have to do far more than use one to throw light on the other; that I was, in fact, compelled to match one rigorously against the other and to draw conclusions about discrepancies; that I would have to build my narrative and analysis from both kinds of sources; that I would have to protect my informants from possible personal or social injury resulting from a public discussion of methodology and sources.

What follows is a more detailed discussion of conditions and factors encountered in field-work and in processing the results of research. Some are cultural in origin and related specifically to the Maori background of my major informants. Others are methodological and could, as I have suggested, arise in any oral history project. It is not always easy to separate the two categories, however; cultural factors that intrude on research and analysis become methodological problems. The approach I shall adopt is to discuss the difficulties that can arise from the preparation for and carrying out of field-work; and then the more purely methodological problems of comparison and analysis.

Work with Maori informants who have been brought up in what could be called a traditional and conservative Maori environment, usually that of a rural Maori community, poses considerations for the researcher beyond the conventional ones of courtesy and copyright. In the first place, if the person or topic to be studied could be viewed as tribal 'property', then it may be necessary to obtain authorisation to proceed from tribal and family sources. There are no ground rules as to how this should be done. The researcher must take prior advice on the appropriate people and organisations to be approached (in some instances it may be enough to see the kaumatua who is regarded as family spokesman, in others it may be necessary to approach a tribal trust board). This is not simply a matter of courtesy, although the courtesy element rates high in Maori consideration; it is also a matter of diplomacy and expedition. Many potential informants will simply not talk about a topic to a stranger if they do not feel that they have tribal or community approval to do so.

In the case of Te Puea, I was helped by the fact that I knew the major informants prior to beginning research, and by the fact that the institution of ariki still operates in Waikato. Once the Arikinui Te Atairangikaahu and Te Puea's immediate family had given permission for my study, most other informants co-operated without question. Without this author- isation, in spite of any personal relationship, they would not have done so.

The researcher who begins without prior relationships will need to take steps to establish rapport with his potential informants. Once authorised to pursue his study, he should make himself known to informants, preferably through a third party known to the researcher and his source; and he should satisfy the informant as to his credentials to proceed, what he intends to do, why, and the use to which the collected research material will be put.

In addition, the researcher must work to establish the kind of relationship in which the informant will feel relaxed and confident enough to answer questions fully and unselfconsciously. This requires not simply the forbearance of the informant but his active co-operation. Apparent ignorance or unwillingness to help are often no more than symptoms of shyness or anxiety. In this context I can do no better than to quote A H Fox Strangways who has said that "willingness is only to be bought with unfeigned sympathy, inexhaustible curiosity, lively gratitude, untiring patience and a scrupulous conscience."

It is also necessary to adopt what Hugh T Tracey has called "personal good manners in the context of local norms". This may mean dressing up for an interview (if it is to begin in a marae situation); or it may require dressing 'down' so as not to provoke discomfort on the part of the informant. In the case of elderly Maori folk it certainly means accepting cups of tea and at least some of the food that is likely to be offered by way of hospitality and decontamination of the tapu state of the traveller. I have noted elsewhere the importance of eating in the home of informants: "The groaning table (euphemistically called 'a cup of tea' but possibly embracing sponges, trifles, fruit salad and cream) has to be dealt with, in spite of work or diets. Eating with people, especially those who do not speak English easily, is the major way of cementing relationships. It gives hosts confidence and makes them happier about discussing more consequential things." I have witnessed the destruction of a potentially close relationship between researcher and informant by a simple and insensitive refusal to accept food. If it really *has* to be refused (and most researchers can summon up the reserves to eat something), then this is best done in what might be called a 'Maori' way, by citing an appropriate proverb, for example ('Ko to te rangatira kai he korero'— 'the food of the rangatira is talk').

Maori language too is an important factor in establishing rapport with the elderly. With reference to the *Tangata Whenua* films I wrote:

"It would be impossible to do this kind of work adequately without some knowledge of spoken Maori: to introduce yourself in acceptable, comprehensible terms; to reply appropriately to formal welcomes; to explain your purpose fully; and (in some cases) to interview non-English speakers. More than any other factor it has been the one that has made the difference between a positive and a negative community response to our overtures. It is also seen as a symptom of sincerity of interest. Doors have been closed in the past because of a literal lack of understanding about people's purpose, or assumed lack of caring deduced from ignorance of basic Maori."

(I have also seen a Maori informant close the door on a researcher because of an innocent misunderstanding of English. The researcher had promised 'generous acknowledgment' of assistance. The informant thought this meant he was to be bribed into co-operation and refused to have any more to do with the researcher.)

Ideally, the researcher of Maori topics should speak fluent Maori. As a bare minimum he should be able to introduce himself in Maori, greet the informant in sincere and courteous terms, explain his purpose, and if necessary ask questions in Maori, even if the informant speaks some English. I reached what I consider to be this minimum level of qualification. Where an informant can speak only Maori or wishes to do so for greater confidence, fluency and clarity, then the non-Maori speaking researcher must have a reliable interpreter and (later) translator, preferably one known to the informant and familiar with local personalities and proper names. I need not emphasise that meticulous care must be taken with subsequent translation and advice sought about ambiguities or uncertainties.

Even after taking all these steps a researcher should leave time for a potential informant to prepare himself and give his contribution some thought, and to investigate the researcher's alleged credentials and the climate of opinion about the proposed project. An interviewee who helped me extensively wrote subsequently: 'Your first letter made me very wary of what was to come as I did not know you personally and I will now confess that I made a special trip to visit Te Ata because without her consent I would never have been able to offer what little I have to give.'

With the groundwork laid, the researcher must make arrangements to return and to begin interviewing. If the informant is elderly, it may be advisable to make arrangements for subsequent visits through a younger and more active member of the family, by telephone or by letter. Experience cautions against arrangements by letter alone, except in the case of younger informants or those with a professional background. It is not uncommon for researchers to arrive for a long-standing interview — perhaps after travelling hundreds of miles — only to find nobody home. It may be that the informant did not understand a letter, was unable to read at all, or simply forgot because the arrangement was made too far in advance and without subsequent confirmation. More important, in the words of a proverb, 'a face seen is a message understood'. It is both more courteous in Maori terms and more prudent to make arrangements in person, if possible. And then it is wise to confirm arrangements through a third party before setting out. Elderly Maori folk are frequently in demand for tangi and hui which may occur at short notice and take them well away from home. The important thing is that when the researcher arrives to work he is expected.

Obviously too the researcher should be well prepared for an interview. He should have read as widely as possible around the topic, consulted previous interviews with other informants, brought copies of relevant documents and photographs for identification, explanation and memory aids, and thought about the interview itself and planned questions. Except in cases where the purpose of the interview is a limited one, the researcher is unlikely to obtain all the information he requires in a single session; he will need to return for elucidation and further questions. Frequently it is only towards the completion of a project that the researcher becomes fully aware of what questions he should be asking.

I have found the use of a tape recorder for interviews essential. Note taking alone is slow and cumbersome. It is difficult to listen carefully to what is being said and to sustain a feeling of conversation if the researcher is looking at his pad and writing throughout. Carefully used, a tape recorder allows informant and researcher simply to talk, comfortably and naturally. Where an informant is unaccustomed to technology he may baulk at the machine and microphone and feel temporarily ill at ease. But this feeling almost always passes with familiarity, especially with the use of a condenser microphone which does not need to be pointed at the speaker.

I have found that most informants talk most satisfactorily in surroundings that are familiar to them, usually their own homes. It is necessary for the interviewer to suggest a quiet place, however, or he may find himself competing with the noises of television, grandchildren or a wet-back stove. Apart from diminishing concentration, such noises-off can seriously affect the audibility of a tape. An empty room is a definite advantage, as is a quiet and comfortable place in a garden.

These things may have to be explained and arranged in advance. Many informants will be accustomed to speaking in noisy public situations, and a family may be tempted to act as spectators to the interview, offering advice or comment. Most often this is not helpful. It can also be surprisingly rewarding to transport an informant to sites where he lived formerly if he is going to talk about them and things that happened there. The sight of forgotten geographical features or derelict buildings can loosen a flood of forgotten recollections, as can the viewing of old photographs.

Numerous and unexpected difficulties will still arise, even in the wake of meticulous preparations for field-work. It is prudent to check that tapes are indeed taping and recorders recording as an interview begins. I have had the experience of finishing an interview with a blank tape, for no apparent reason. More commonly, the informant may not be close enough to be audible or some other noise may be causing interference. It is far easier to check these things at the outset than it is to repeat a lengthy and possibly exhausting conversation, although it is wise not to cut a speaker off in full stride to do this (a simple test conversation, explained as such, is adequate).

Sometimes it may be necessary to improvise unorthodox tactics to secure co-operation. One informant was initially unwilling to be part of the project, in spite of its being authorised by Te Atairangikaahu. What finally induced him to co-operate was the information that other people were placing on record their view of his contribution to the Kingitanga; he was in effect being represented to posterity by other spokesmen, and this proved unacceptable to him. He began to work with me to correct what he considered to be the misconceptions of others.

The pattern of the interview itself will be determined by the kind of rapport that the researcher has established with the informant, and by the informant's willingness to communicate. It should be structured in the sense that the researcher should have as clear an idea as possible of the ground he wants to cover; but it is unlikely to proceed satisfactorily if the researcher sticks to his plan like a script. Obviously, an informant will talk most freely and most fully if he is at ease.

Interrogative interviewing is unlikely to be appropriate for elderly Maori informants. It is usually more satisfactory for the interviewer to nominate the subject he wishes the interviewee to talk about and then let him discourse about it, waikorero style. Interruptions should be minimal and certainly not such as to break the interviewee's flow of thought or narrative (interruption of an elder on what could be regarded as a formal occasion is looked upon far more unfavourably in Maori circles than in Pakeha ones). As the informant is talking, the interviewer can jot down questions about matters which are not clear or which could benefit from elaboration. In addition, he should be crossing off topics as they are covered from his check list. Additional questions should be raised after the speaker has completed his peroration.

Observations made in the course of the *Tangata Whenua* series are applicable in this context. I noted that the interviewer may have to discard his own notions of time and relevance. "It's partly because of a rural mode of communication, partly a Maori one. There is a strong suspicion and dislike of the city hustler who breezes in with preconceived ideas and tries to mould people. The tempo that works is a bit like the one you adopt for a tolls operator: 'transfer charge, person to person, number calling, person calling, number charged to, number calling from, who's calling'— if you break the sequence or accelerate the pace you destroy the rhythm and communication [may collapse] . . . Within the right tempo, you may have to approach the subject of conversation in slow concentric circles, deal with it, and back out gradually the way you came in."

I should add, however, that there are no sure recipes for interviews of this kind. The most a researcher can do is anticipate the conditions he may encounter, be aware of how other people have coped with them, and then rely on sensitivity and intuition.

Inevitably, some reputable informants turn out to be blusterers. Hours and hours of talking may produce only a massive willingness to help and to be part of the historical record — but no useful first-hand information nor helpful insights shed on the topics discussed. Others of my informants, even more difficult, appeared at first to be blusterers but turned out to be storehouses of information. There is need to be as careful in the rejection of informants as in their selection.

An initial difficulty with some informants was their predisposition to say what they thought they should say in answer to my question, to present a 'sanitised' view of protagonists and relationships (this sprang from the fact that many informants assumed at the outset that the purpose of the exercise was to gather panegyrics for Te Puea and other leaders of the past). Early in discussion I asked Tumokai Katipa about a vital relationship in Te Puea's life, that with Apirana Ngata. "She thought he was a very nice man," Katipa said cautiously. "Very clever too." Much later, in the course of discussing specific topics like the opening of Mahinarangi and the beginning of the land development schemes, a far more complex view emerged. The only questions in this context that had any real meaning were ones like: "What did Ngata say at the opening of Raukawa and what did Te Puea think about that?" Broad queries most often did not produce useful information. They were worth asking mainly as an entrance to more detailed conversation.

A related difficulty was that some informants believed throughout the project that its purpose (and the purpose of their talking to me) was to manifest and uplift the joint mana of Te Puea and the Kingitanga. This meant that they were unwilling to discuss some vitally important issues and incidents if they felt that information about them would reflect discredit on Te Puea, Tainui or the King Movement. Usually such matters involved sex, alcohol or money (Te Puea's promiscuous behaviour in early years was an example). In such cases I had to agree to respect confidences, to seek verification from other informants less unwilling to be identified, or simply not to acknowledge my source so as to protect an informant from personal or social injury.

Where I felt that information was titillating but not central to an understanding of personalities or issues, I made no reference to it — although I left such information on tapes for the possible use of later researchers. If on the other hand I thought that the information was germane — as in the case of Henare Kaihau's alleged relationship with Mahuta's wife — then I referred to it in discreet terms.

Discretion did not prevent violent reaction from some people, however. A woman who had read my description of Te Puea's early years was highly offended and said: "You've written about things that people have no right to write about." (Like many of my Maori advisers, she made distinctions between what was appropriate for oral transmission among Maori and what was appropriate for preservation on the written record for anyone to see; she viewed the former situation as the arena for scrutiny and criticism, and the latter as the proper place for closed-ranked tribute and adulation.) I found the only way to disarm this sort of criticism was to give some indication of the kinds of things I had chosen *not* to write about — to emphasise the fact that I had indeed been both selective and discreet.

The foregoing raises a diverting but interesting question. Is it easier for a Maori than for a Pakeha to write 'Maori history', particularly a Maori from the tribe or family concerned? This suggestion has been made with confidence. From my own experience I would contend that it is not so, at least certainly not straightforwardly so. The outsider — especially the Pakeha who is known locally and trusted and made privy to 'inside' information — is often more easily able to cope with many of the factors discussed above because he is not as bound by Maori expectations as a Maori would be; nor is he expected to be subject to what might be called 'Maori consequences' for such things as not upholding mana or encroaching on matters regarded as tapu. And it seems to me to be essential for an understanding of some matters that the truth is able to be told and not concealed for reasons of culture or diplomacy.

Even the Pakeha researcher who limits his discussions scrupulously to matters of relevance and weighs information carefully and responsibly will encounter difficulties of a purely Maori kind. Following publication of *Te Puea*, I received a letter which said in part: "The Kaihau family have been deeply wounded by the way they come out in this book. Even small children have been humiliated, and older ones thrown into despair . . . In dealing with Maori things we have to remember that nga mahi o nga tipuna [the doings of ancestors] have a place in contemporary life . . . you can't make a separation of generations . . . you must consider the effect on the living." The letter went on to suggest that I should apologise to the Kaihau, Herewini and Tamehana families for including in the book information about their forebears that could be regarded as discreditable. There is no suggestion that the information is incorrect, or even unfair; simply that it will make it difficult for descendants to hold their heads up because of their oneness with ancestors. All this compounds the historian's conventional difficulties of selection and discretion and may make it difficult for him to return to an earlier area of research.

It also seems to me to be unrealistically idealistic to state that Maori groups are more likely to arrive at agreement on one Maori candidate for a project than on a Pakeha. Would Ngai Porou reach an easy consensus about which East Coaster was best qualified to write about Ngata? Or Taranaki on a candidate for Te Whiti O Rongomai? From the way both federations speak about such matters, it seems unlikely. If the candidate were local, his case would be subject to inter-family and sub-tribal tensions, and to the often cruel refusal to accept a local prophet in his own country. And if it were a case of a Maori candidate from another district, there would be strong suspicions about his motives for moving outside his own people (such as an East Coaster raised when he approached Waikato for permission to write an MA thesis on the institution of poukai).

I did encounter occasional difficulty extracting information on matters considered tapu or religious. To throw light on this and related aspects of research, I want to quote at some length from an earlier discussion of mine, about conservative Maori attitudes to documents and the process of converting oral traditions to documentary or literary forms:

". . . the process of conveying information was formerly surrounded by religious concepts. It is still thus supported in the cosmology that many Maori adopt when they move out of a Pakeha situation into a Maori one. There is still a tradition among older people that once you have committed information to memory in appropriate and authorised circumstances, then that information with a life of its own becomes part of you and your life. In particular it becomes part of your mauri and part of your personal tapu, the quality that protects. John Rangihau of Tuhoe explains the feeling this way:

"'I talk about mauri and some people talk about tapu. Perhaps the words are interchangeable. If you apply this life-force feeling to all things — inanimate and animate — and to concepts, and give each concept a life of its own, you can see how difficult it appears for older people to be willing and available to give out information. They believe it is part of them, part of their own life-force, and when they start shedding this they are giving away themselves. Only when they depart are they able to pass this whole thing through and give it a continuing character. Just as they are proud of being able to trace their genealogy backwards, in the same way they can continue to send the mauri of certain things forward.'

"A consequence of accepting this view is that you may say or re-tell certain things (particularly tauparapara, whakapapa, or family stories) only in circumstances that are appropriate — usually hui, tangi or whare wananga. Misuse of information can make its sacred character profane. It can result in a diminution of mauri (which Rangihau says leaves a person 'an empty hulk' and 'without purpose'). And it can create chinks in the armour of personal tapu, leaving a man vulnerable to physical and mental illness. It can even bring about death . . . many Maori sources believe, on first reaction, that by committing information to paper, tape or film they are risking illness or misfortune."

I encountered a number of problems in the course of the *Te Puea* project that arose out of such attitudes and values.

One was a tremendous reverence for anything written by Te Puea, coupled with a strong feeling that anything written by her or others for private consumption (diary, letters to private correspondents) was not appropriate for public consumption. At the request of one informant I withdrew references from letters written in the 1930s, mainly about conditions at Waahi Pa. But the attitude was most obtrusively associated with Te Puea's diary. This document is a proverbial mine of information and one that, knowledgeably and sympathetically edited, should make a book on its own. It includes not only details of her movements over thirty years, but also her intelligent assessment of the affairs of the day, and in particular her frequent observations about the behaviour of other public figures.

Attitudes to publication of the diary were — at the time of writing — insurmountably conservative. One view is that it is a tapu document (like King Te Rata's journal held in the Pei Jones Papers) and therefore not suitable for publication (and there was a great deal of resentment among some Waikato kaumatua when Pei Te Hurinui referred to Te Rata's journal in his essay, 'Maori Kings'). There was another and what might be termed 'Pakeha' view that the diary should never be published because it was not written for publication. It contains information of an intimate and highly confidential nature about some people still living and others only recently dead. The informant primarily responsible for the diary, Alex McKay, was unable to answer to his own or to my satisfaction the question why Te Puea kept it in the first place. His eventual and reluctantly expressed view was that this activity was "compulsive". An additional difficulty he raised was that of the initials, other abbreviations and personal short-hand references that Te Puea used and which he believed could be understood only by Pei Te Hurinui and in some instances himself. Once McKay is no longer available, editing of the document will be extremely difficult.

A related difficulty was a fear among some elderly informants that there could be consequences of a traditional kind for talking with me, and that a life would have to be paid as a price for completion of the project. Some earlier reservations were removed by the instruction of Te Atairangikaahu that kaumatua were to help me, and that their actions would not then come into the category of hara, and involve loss of personal tapu. But the fear of loss of life was strong, as it had been on other projects with which I have been associated. One informant, aware of this feeling, indicated he was prepared to be the lightning rod for such consequences. He knew what people were saying, he believed in the validity of what they said, and he knew he was dying in the year that he helped me. There was a noticeable relaxation among some other informants in the wake of his death in 1975.

One other matter should be mentioned. I frequently and unexpectedly turned up useful documentary material by asking interviewees if they had photographs, letters, newspaper clippings or things of this kind. The private papers of Mick Jones and Maharaia Winiata came to light in this way. Such documents were also to be found on a smaller scale in homes where I had no reason to look for them. Many families, for example, kept a record of deaths and tangi. This can be invaluable as a means of dating events that might otherwise be fixed only by their proximity to other events.

I have referred to the need to check oral evidence rigorously against documentary sources, where possible. There were many points at which I found the oral and documentary records differed. In some cases it was because the documentary source was incorrect. And, as I have said elsewhere, errors conceived by careless or uncomprehending researchers tend to be perpetuated merely because they have acquired documentary authority.

One of the most emphatic examples I can give is Eric Ramsden's belief that Te Puea was responsible for some of the carving at the front of Pare Waikato, the meeting house completed in 1927. Everybody I spoke to who lived in or close to Turangawaewae in the 1920s was adamant that Te Puea never touched the pare or maihi of this house, other than to give directions on how she wanted it done; and that she never carved facings for any building, believing very strongly that this was work for men only. To doubt this view I would have to suspect a conscious conspiracy on the part of the inhabitants of Turangawaewae to cover up a public event that would have been witnessed by dozens of people and talked about by hundreds more; and I cannot believe this to be the case.

Ramsden appears to have misunderstood a remark of Te Puea's when he first visited Turangawaewae in August 1927. Certainly this was his first meeting with Te Puea, and probably his first discussion with a group of Maori in a Maori situation. The ground was fertile for misunderstanding. As a result of the visit Ramsden wrote: "Visitors are housed in the capacious and well-ventilated meeting house, part of the carving for which the Princess did herself."

Nearly thirty years later, W J Phillipps perpetuated and compounded the error and attributed it to a communication with Ramsden when he wrote that Pare Waikato was "built under the instruction of Princess Te Puea Herangi, who carved the pare over the door. The maihi was carved by a professional carver, later to be dismissed by Te Puea, who completed the work herself." The assertion appeared again in 1975. Anne Salmond wrote in *Hui* that "Princess te Puea [sic] dismissed a professional carver working on the house Waikato at Turangawaewae marae, and completed the door architrave herself." The information was attributed to Phillipps. In 1977, the same assertion appeared in John Cresswell's *Maori Meeting Houses of the North Island*: "Princess Te Puea Herangi directed the construction of this house, and, after dismissing the professional carvers, completed the maihi and carved door pare herself." All these references have attracted more than passing interest because there is only one other apparently documented case of a woman working on meeting house carvings; and they illustrate how difficult it is to correct an error once it has appeared in print.

Conversely, the oral and documentary records sometimes differed because the oral record was demonstrably incorrect. There appeared to be four principal ways in which this could happen.

The first was a straight out failure of memory. Occasionally — and understandably — the passage of time obscured recollection, and people either could not remember things they witnessed, or they remembered them inaccurately. There is nothing sinister about this process; the researcher has simply to be aware and wary of it. I was assured by one woman who remembered Tawhiao and had attended his tangi that the prophet King had had no facial moko. This was quite clearly disproved, of course, by photographs and the recorded recollections of others.

Second, stories sometimes became confused or incorrect in detail as a result of transmission through more than one person. One example is an account of the occasion on which a woman exposed herself to Maui Pomare during the Waikato anti-conscription campaign. One informant recalled Te Puea saying that Pomare had been accompanied by Sir James Carroll and that it was Carroll who proved himself a "true rangatira" by not shielding himself from the spectacle. Ramsden's account written from Te Puea's mouth thirty years earlier makes it clear that the companion who so distinguished himself was Te Heuheu Tukino. This was confirmed by a letter to Ramsden from Lady Pomare.

Third, distortion may occur as a result of the wish of an informant to appear in a more favourable light (and this wish and the resulting errors may be wholly unconscious). Late in 1974 an informant told me Te Puea had not opposed enlistment in the 1914-1918 war. I was unable to comprehend the utter discrepancy of this account with the documentary record until it was pointed out to me by Pei Te Hurinui that this informant was one of the few who had agreed to take a uniform and train for army services after his arrest, that he wanted to justify his decision, and that he had no idea of the extent of my information from other sources.

Fourth, stories seemed sometimes to have altered in transmission because of the wish of the story-teller to point up maxims and morals. One example is the popular account (in the 1970s) of Te Puea's investiture in 1937 that has her walking forward to receive her CBE in working boots. Photographs of the occasion show her to be wearing carpet slippers; the origin of the working boots version would appear to be the wish to emphasise her attitude to Pakeha formalities and her own industry, which kept her at manual tasks even through the most ceremonious of events.

There were occasions, of course, when I would very much have liked to compare oral and documentary records but was unable to do so because of the absence of one or the other. There were no longer eyewitnesses to the events that caused Te Puea to abandon Roy Secombe and return to Waikato in 1910, for example. Here I had to lean more heavily than I wanted on the rather romantic story compiled by Judge Acheson. This was a pivotal point in Te Puea's life for which I would have preferred a direct account.

On other occasions, when oral accounts were available but not sufficiently detailed for my needs, I was able to fill them out with minutiae gleaned from documents (the daily routine on the land development schemes, for example). But I attempted to distribute weight and emphasis according to the criteria of surviving participants. Conversely, there were occasions where reliable oral accounts were available for key incidents that were most unlikely to be verified against documentary evidence. One example was the conversation between Te Puea and Michael Joseph Savage over the appointment of George Shepherd to the Native Land Court. This was witnessed by Pei Te Hurinui, whom I considered a reliable witness; such closed-door decisions are unlikely to be noted in government archival material.

One constant factor was the desirability of making comparisons between Te Puea and Waikato, and leaders from other tribal areas. I was unable to do this to anything like the extent that I would have liked. There was relatively little supporting information in print, although I made use of what there was. The diplomatic difficulties of extracting material from other living sources in the manner I was doing in Waikato were immense and time-consuming. Not only did rapport with Waikato not help to obtain similar assistance from other areas, in some cases it was a positive disadvantage.

The greatest single methodological difficulty I encountered was deciding what the relationship should be between the interviews I had conducted and the published comments drawn from those interviews. Previous work had given me views on this matter and some experience in the business of interviewing, editing and referral back to sources. Hence I began with the following assumptions.

(1) It was advisable to interview informants in as wide-ranging a manner as possible — both for their own comfort (so they did not feel pushed about or restricted in what they could say) and to gather as much information as I could about as many topics and events as possible. I was acutely aware that elderly informants were unlikely to be interviewed again; and that though my reason and excuse for interviewing them was Te Puea's life, they were able and willing to talk with authority about many aspects of early 20th century Maori life. When they strayed into details or topics that were not germane to my subject, therefore, I did not divert them. I was aware that there would be other researchers who would one day want to pursue this material. It seemed valuable to collect on tape everything that was offered.

(2) Most of them could not be quoted verbatim in references of more than one sentence. There is, clearly, an enormous difference between oral and literary modes of communication; and oral history, to some extent, sets out to make literary what was formerly oral. Verbatim quotes of any length on relevant topics would be likely to include references to cups of tea, dogs barking, children's misbehaviour, looking for mislaid false teeth; as well as the stammerings, hesitations and nonsequiturs of ordinary speech. In addition, old people frequently do not talk chronologically; their attention wanders and they often repeat themselves. Sometimes they talk more lucidly about a topic the second time they refer to it; sometimes they are most intelligible in the first half of the first reference and the second half of the second reference.

None of this should invalidate what they say or preclude a researcher from quoting his informants. Nor should it require the researcher to quote them in such a way as to make them sound mentally defective or senile. The simple consequence is that editing is necessary and justifiable — to establish degrees of coherence and clarity appropriate to the project; and to eliminate irrelevancies and repetitions. (Willa K Baum has noted, however, that the nature of editing should vary according to the purpose of a researcher's programme. If he is attempting to explore the thought process of a one-hundred-and-four-year-old, or a poet's stream-of-consciousness, then editing may be undesirable, or at least of a different kind.) Editing may also be necessary to ensure that informants are represented to posterity in a manner in which they and their families would approve; I considered this a necessary ethical assumption linked to what Baum has referred to as the ability of an oral history project "to bestow a feeling of recognition and dignity on the older members of the community".

(3) Having edited those sections of the interviews from which I wished to quote, I felt an obligation to refer the resulting transcript back to informants to assist accuracy and clarity and to test their satisfaction with the manner in which they were to be quoted.

All this came within the terms of my original ideal of an oral history project and seemed straightforward. In practice, however, it was anything but that:

(1) In the first place, the lengths of some of my interviews (especially those with Tumokai Katipa and Piri Poutapu) were prodigious. It would have taken over a year of full-time work simply to transcribe the tapes in full. (It has been estimated that one and a half hours of taped interview generates forty hours of processing; and one hundred hours two years. Willa Baum notes that thirty taped hours fully transcribed is likely to produce nine hundred pages of transcript. Needless to say the University of Waikato was unable to supply a person with a good knowledge of written and spoken Maori in addition to transcribing and typing skills.)

(2) To listen to all the tapes and transcribe and edit only those sections that I wanted to use (a fraction of the total) took over six months. In this manner, doing what could be considered the bare minimum of processing, I typed what seemed to be the most relevant sections of the interviews, edited them, and referred them to my informants. Frequently matters that did not at first seem important would assume significance subsequently, especially matters requiring cross-references, and I would have to listen to many more hours of tape, locate the new sections, type and edit them, and then relate them to what I had already typed.

(3) Edited material referred back to sources frequently generated subsequent discussion and fresh information as a result of further consideration and jogging of the informant's memory. The process sometimes produced second-thoughts in which the informants became alarmed at the baldness of what they had first said; it sometimes produced an outright contradiction — a claim that what was quoted had not been

said at all. All these reactions produced a need to further rewrite the edited transcripts.

The result of all these factors was that in some instances (although by no means the majority) final passages for quotation bore only indirect resemblance to the original verbatim comments. The consequence was most often an improvement in detail and clarity; but on a number of occasions I was concerned that vigour was lost and emphases changed. It was an unavoidable consequence of committing myself to refer material back to major informants before quotation and attribution. In future projects I would do this, but not as a matter of right, and not giving the informant discretion to alter material on any grounds other than factual ones.

Baum has noted wryly that "There is much disagreement in oral history circles on what should and should not be done in the way of editing." This is understating the situation. At the time of writing there were no accepted rules of evidence as in the case of court procedure or in the methodology of conventional documentary history. Viewing the *Te Puea* project in retrospect, however, the most satisfactory course of procedure for future projects would seem to be this:

All tapes should be kept. In addition to their information value, there will be interest in accent, inflection, speech patterns, significant hesitations and the degree of emotion with which an informant may infuse his recollection — what could be called the 'flavour' of the interview and the interviewee. As Baum suggests, such tapes should be marked with the name of the interviewer, the project title, the number of the session (first, second, etc), and the length.

Verbatim transcripts should be typed and one copy filed.

The second copy should be edited by the interviewer, retyped, and sent or taken to the informant. This document should then be returned to the interviewer with the informant's changes and comments noted. (If the informant is illiterate or infirm, the interviewer may find it necessary to note these things at the direction of the informant.) On this document, preferably in a different coloured ink, the interviewer should also note the changes initiated by the informant and comment on them where they appear significant.

The interviewer should then type a third document incorporating the alterations, this to be used for quotation and attribution. It should not be referred to the informant, except in the case of serious doubts or ambiguities.

All three written copies of the interviews should be identified (in order of preparation) and kept so that the record shows clearly the process by which original material became quotable and quoted. Both the original verbatim transcript and the final edited document should have numbered pages, an index with a list of subjects discussed, and (ideally) cross-references.

None of this is accomplished easily or speedily. In the case of a major project it is a laborious and time-consuming process well beyond the resources of an individual researcher. It requires a back-up institution to prepare transcripts and do much of the re-typing. Ideally, processing should be carried out by full-time specialists in an institution to which the individual researcher would attach himself for the duration of the project. Less ideally, any institution sponsoring future oral history projects (a university, a library, the Queen Elizabeth II Arts council, for example) *must* make provision either for the typing of transcripts by professionals; or for sufficient funding for the researcher to arrange for this to be done.

Baum suggests that a written agreement should be drawn up between interviewer and informant, and that it should include conditions for the release of the interview material. I would agree. In the case of the *Te Puea* project, tapes and partial transcripts were deposited with the Alexander Turnbull Library with the condition that they were not to be consulted or quoted without the permission of the interviewer and Dame Te Atairangi-kaahu (representing Waikato interests and Te Puea's family).

It would be advisable for thought to be given to such matters before interviews begin, particularly if they are likely to include sensitive or controversial material; and if a declared restriction is likely to make an informant more relaxed about speaking fully and frankly. In some instances it may be necessary to consider an embargo against publication until after the death of the informant or the people of whom he is speaking.

Some consideration too should be given in the review of copyright law to provisions that meet the new factors raised by oral history: should copyright lie with the interviewer, the interviewee, the institution holding the transcripts, or should it be distributed among all three? (Tom Wilsted of the Alexander Turnbull Library has suggested it should rest primarily with the holding institution because of its more informed idea of potential usage.)

If one single thing is clear from all I have said, it is surely that oral history offers no short cuts to an understanding of the past. The view that truth is to be harvested rapidly and excitingly by rushing into the field with tape recorders and talking to anybody with relevant recollections is romantic; as is the belief that this process is in some way 'easier' than working with documents. True, documents do not talk back and oral informants do; but both factors have in-built handicaps.

Subjects who do talk back, who distill what they say through passion, prejudice and memory, are infinitely more difficult and time-consuming to work with and to cross-check than are documents; and the real work — the processing that excavates probability, insight and interpretation — continues long after the heady experience of tracking down informants and interviewing them.